Carl Hentsch

New York Beauties
& FLYING GEESE

10 Dramatic Quilts, 27 Pillows, 31 Block Patterns

C&T PUBLISHING

Acknowledgments

Thank you to everyone who quilted for me (in no particular order): Teresa Silva, Karen McTavish, Kelly Cline, Angela Walters, Mary Verstraete Honas, and Frank Palmer.

A huge thank-you to Tula Pink for all her encouragement, support, and color wizardry!

Thank you to my team at C&T for getting me though the process.

And finally, thank you to Art Gallery Fabrics, FreeSpirit Fabric, RJR Fabrics, Tula Pink, and Westminster Fibers for providing fabric when I needed it.

Publisher: Amy Marson

Creative Director: Gailen Runge

Editor: Karla Menaugh

Technical Editors: Debbie Rodgers and Amanda Siegfried

Cover/Book Designer: Page+Pixel

Production Coordinator / Illustrator: Tim Manibusan

Production Editor: Alice Mace Nakanishi

Photo Assistant: Carly Jean Marin

Photography by Diane Pedersen of C&T Publishing, Inc., unless otherwise noted

Published by C&T Publishing, Inc., P.O. Box 1456, Lafayette, CA 94549

Library of Congress Cataloging-in-Publication Data

Names: Hentsch, Carl, author.

Title: New York beauties & flying geese : 10 dramatic quilts, 27 pillows, 31 block patterns / Carl Hentsch.

Other titles: New York beauties and flying geese

Description: Lafayette, California : C&T Publishing, Inc., [2017] | Includes index.

Identifiers: LCCN 2016037647 | ISBN 9781617451768 (soft cover)

Subjects: LCSH: Patchwork--Patterns. | Quilting--Patterns. | New York beauty quilts.

Classification: LCC TT835 .H4445 2017 | DDC 746.46--dc23

LC record available at https://lccn.loc.gov/2016037647

Printed in the USA

10 9 8 7 6 5 4

Contents

19 THE PROJECTS — Bonus! A quilt project and a pillow project for each design!

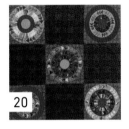
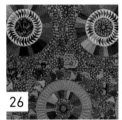

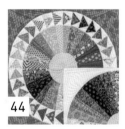

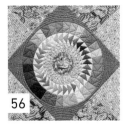

A Note from Tula

I met Carl several years ago at our local quilt shop, which just happened to be a favorite local hangout for both of us. It didn't take me very long to get really curious about this guy who quietly walked the floor making the most unpredictable fabric choices week after week. While most people shopped primarily in one general section of the store, Carl was interested in a little bit of everything. Like any regular fabric store dweller, I was dying to know what he was making with all this fabric! It was a few weeks later when he brought his first quilt tops in to the shop to be quilted. I don't know exactly what I was expecting, but it wasn't this. They were startlingly complex and architectural. Everyone present at the shop that day spent the next several minutes just staring at these pieced works of art in complete awe. I believe the first thing I ever said to him was, "Who are you?" in a joking but accusatory manner, which pretty much set the tone for the friendship that we would build over the coming years—a friendship that mostly consisted of him showing me things he was working on and me telling him that he was crazy.

Carl and I are opposites in our craft in almost every way. Carl thinks of a quilt in terms of piecing, and I think of a quilt in terms of fabric selection. In essence we are yin and yang when it comes to piecing and quilting. When Carl showed me the sketches for the quilts that would eventually be featured in this book, I was mesmerized. These were the quilts that I wished I could design but knew I never would and probably never could. I desperately wanted to watch these quilts develop and see how they would change from the first page to the last page. So, naturally, I gave unsolicited advice. That evening I began pulling fabrics and texting him pictures of the fabrics I thought he should use. A conversation began, followed shortly by weekly trips to the fabric store, just like old times. I have never had so much fun talking about, selecting, and arranging fabrics.

In these pages Carl has created something that speaks directly to the character of quilting today. He has taken one very specific idea and explored it from every angle, creating a single, totally complete thought. What I love about these quilts is that they are caught, like so many of us right now, in the gray area between traditional and modern quilting—that undefinable space between a time-honored craft and a burgeoning art form, between yesterday and tomorrow. Instead of shying away from that gray area, he has embraced it.

In their rawest form, these quilts speak to a sort of deconstructed traditionalism, taking cues from blocks that most quilters are familiar with but with the blocks taken apart and reassembled in exciting new ways. An interchangeable block that can be broken down and taken apart in so many ways is what quilting is all about today. It is about choices and it is about the maker, not the author, putting his or her own personality and creativity into every project. Quilting is personal.

Carl has created quilts here that are aspirational. At a time when beginning quilters are becoming more confident and longtime quilters are indulging the desire to make quilts that take full advantage of their skills, here is a book that asks the maker to see more than boundaries and categories, to think beyond the usual choices, and to make something exceptional.

xx,

Tula

Tula Pink is an illustrator, fabric designer, quilter, and author. She designs fabrics for FreeSpirit Fabric, is a BERNINA Ambassador, and has designed thread and ribbon collections for Aurifil and Renaissance Ribbons.

66 These were the quilts that I wished I could design but knew I never would and probably never could. 99
—Tula

Introduction

This book combines a few of my favorite things—foundation piecing, curved piecing, New York Beauty blocks, and Flying Geese. I wanted to create quilts that had standard building blocks—pieced arcs, plain arcs, and fans—that could be mixed and matched in a variety of ways.

My initial concept was to have the Flying Geese in black and eight other fabrics repeating around the circle. I jumped at the chance when Tula Pink wanted to have a part in the book. Collaborating with her was a great opportunity for me to learn more about fabric and color choices—knowledge that I have carried forward to other projects.

After I showed my ideas to Tula, the quilts blossomed into full color. It was a great pleasure having Tula offer suggestions and guide me along the way. You can read more about that in Fabric—The Basic Ingredient (page 8).

The most important ingredient in any quilt is the fabric, and we carefully chose the fabrics in each quilt to go with the quilt design and its position in the book. The quilts featured in this book tell a color story from beginning to end, starting with bright jewel tones in *Floating Orbs* (page 20) and fading to white in *Wedding Cake* (page 72). As I selected the fabrics, the designs took shape and the quilts began to take on lives of their own.

Though these quilts may look complicated, you can make them with some uncomplicated foundation-piecing and curved-piecing techniques. If you are new to foundation piecing and curved piecing, I think you will find that your skills will improve very rapidly as you become more familiar with these techniques.

The Basics section (starting on next page) shows you how to make fabric decisions, as well as how to master the cutting and stitching techniques. If you want to experiment first before starting a full quilt, try making a pillow or two. The pillows will give you a chance to try out your own color choices and to perfect your foundation-piecing and curved-piecing skills. Before long, you will have your own gorgeous quilt or pillow!

The Basics

Choosing Fabrics and Thread

Fabric—The Basic Ingredient

The quilts in this book are made from fabric groupings of 8, 24, or 32 colors for foundation-pieced geese and fan arcs. Of course, the more fabrics you use, the more of a rainbow effect you can create.

So where do you start when wandering the aisles among the many bolts of fabric in your local quilt shop?

PRECUTS

The easiest place to start is with a precut fat-quarter bundle. These bundles typically consist of all the fabrics from a line produced by a fabric designer or a selection of fabrics chosen by the designer that go well together. *Pandemonium* (page 26) and *Sorbet* (page 60) started out as fat-quarter bundles of shot cottons. Don't be afraid, though, to move the fabrics around or add or subtract other colors that you may prefer. From there you can add coordinating prints or solids to complete your fabric selections.

PRINTS

Solids or shot cottons work great, but don't be afraid of a print either. Take a look at *Floating Orbs* (page 20) and *Crazy Tula* (page 44). I used both medium- and smaller-scale prints for the pieced arcs in these quilts. You just want to make sure that when you are cutting up these fabrics, you won't end up with pieces that appear as a single color.

POLKA DOTS

Polka dots are another favorite of mine. With *Seeing Spots* (page 50), I was able to coordinate 32 different fabrics from Kaffe Fassett's collection for Westminster Fibers.

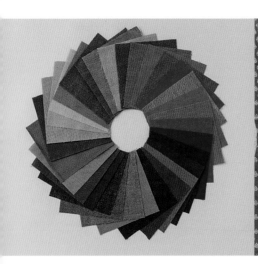
Fabric selection for *Pandemonium* (page 26)

Close-up of *Crazy Tula* (page 44)

Fabric choices for *Seeing Spots* (page 50)

BACKGROUNDS

The next step is to choose the coordinating background pieces. These fabric selections will depend on what you have chosen for the arcs. If you chose solids for the geese and fans, choose prints for the pieced backgrounds. If you chose prints for the arcs, use solids for the background. Don't be worried if some of the arc fabrics begin to blend with the background fabrics. This will add dimension and sparkle to the quilt, especially when you use different colors for each ring of the background.

WORKING YOUR STASH

With few exceptions, each of my quilts features fabrics from one designer or fabric company. However, sometimes you just need to reach into your stash of fabrics and combine things you love.

Papyrus (page 66) is a great example. One night I went to Tula's house with several boxes of neutral fabrics that I had pulled from my stash— some yardage but mostly fat quarters. She has this quirk about her where she needs to put fabrics in order, and in no time I had the fabrics chosen for the quilt. Another quilt for which this worked well was *Rust* (page 38), where I combined multiple designer fabrics.

CHOOSING A THEME

In my journey for this book, I learned valuable lessons from Tula. Choosing a theme and selecting fabrics from the same designer, even if you are crossing fabric lines, increases the probability of success for a novice such as myself.

BIG, BOLD PRINTS

And finally, don't be afraid of big, bold prints. Choose the largest-print background fabrics to coordinate and use as many of the colors as possible in the rings. Don't worry about how you cut the fabrics, as the background pieces to complete the blocks are large. When the blocks are assembled, they provide another dimension to the quilt.

Close-up of *Pandemonium* (page 26)   Close-up of *Rust* (page 38)   Close-up of *Sorbet* (page 60)

Thread Selection—Holding It All Together

If the fabric is like the flour, then I consider the thread to be like the wet ingredients in a cake that hold it all together. I have tried a variety of threads in my quest to perfect my foundation piecing. I prefer a strong, thin thread, as I find that reduces any bulges or bumps in my piecing.

My two favorite go-to threads are Aurifil 50-weight cotton and WonderFil DecoBob 80-weight polyester. Both of these threads are strong and will stand up to the removal of the foundation papers. Be sure to stick with a single brand on any one quilt.

Making the Blocks

The block designs are variations of the New York Beauty block, constructed in quarter-blocks. Each quarter-block is made of one, two, or three interchangeable arcs, each either pieced or cut from a single fabric. The quarter-block is completed with a center quarter-circle and an outer background piece that sets the arcs into a square block.

The Block Index (page 76) shows the patterns for 31 different blocks you can make by switching out the arc combinations.

Sometimes you will set the center quarter-circles into the block with curved piecing. Other times you will sew some of the quarter-blocks together first and replace the quarter-circle with an appliquéd half-circle or full circle.

To make the blocks, follow these basic instructions, referring to Foundation Piecing (page 12), Curved Piecing (page 16), and Appliquéd Center Circles (page 17) for more detailed information.

1. Copy the foundation-piecing patterns for your project. In the materials list near the beginning of each project chapter, you will find a section called Foundations and Patterns. That section lists the arcs for which you will need foundation-piecing patterns. Photocopy (or scan and print) the listed number of foundation patterns for each arc.

2. Make plastic templates for the background, circle, and plain arc patterns you will need, also listed in Foundations and Patterns.

3. Cut the fabric pieces for your quilt. Refer to the Cutting section of the project to see how many pieces you should cut from each fabric. See Cutting Pieces for the Blocks (next page) in this chapter for detailed instructions on how to prepare the fabric pieces.

4. Stitch the foundation-pieced arcs, following the instructions in Foundation Piecing (page 12).

If your blocks need to follow an exact pattern, the project instructions will tell you which blocks to use from the Block Index (page 76) and will include a block layout diagram. If not, you'll be able to mix and match pieced and plain arcs as you wish. The quilt photo and quilt assembly diagram will give you further information about color placement.

5. Sew the elements of each block together, following the instructions in Curved Piecing (page 16). Many of the blocks are sewn in quarter sections first. The project instructions will give you more detailed information.

Cutting Pieces for the Blocks

In each project, you'll find instructions for the number of pieces to cut for each part of the quilt—the pieced arcs as well as the backgrounds; circles, half-circles, or quarter-circles; and plain arcs.

FOUNDATION-PIECED ARCS

To see which arc pieces you will need, refer to Block Index (page 76) and Foundation-Pieced Arc Patterns (page 84). Using the cutting chart (below right), refer to the project instructions for your quilt to see how many pieces to cut.

For all the foundation-pieced segments, you will start with slightly oversized triangles and rectangles that you will trim as you stitch each arc.

For the Flying Geese arcs—A, B, and C—cut half-square triangles from background fabrics and feature fabrics. Cut the same size of triangle for both, even though the finished size on the backgrounds will be smaller than the "geese."

For the remaining arc designs, cut rectangular shapes.

BACKGROUNDS, PLAIN ARCS, AND CIRCLES

To see which pieces you will need, refer to the Block Index (page 76). Make a plastic template for each pattern piece. Using the cutting chart (at right), refer to the project instructions for your quilt to see how many pieces to cut.

Cutting Shapes with Templates

1. Trace each pattern onto sturdy template plastic and cut out with scissors (*not* your fabric scissors!).

2. For each shape, precut the necessary fabric squares or rectangles as indicated in Precutting for Template Shapes (page 12).

> ▶ To make the J pieces, trace the J1 full circle, J2 half-circle, or J3 quarter-circle onto the square or rectangle indicated and cut out with scissors.

> ▶ To make the K and K-reverse background pieces, place the 4″ fabric strip wrong side up. You will be able to trace 6 of the K background pieces onto a single width-of-fabric strip. Flip the template over and repeat on another strip to make 6 of the K-reverse background pieces.

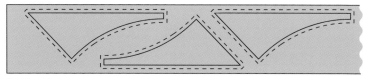

Cutting K pieces

---

tip ▶▶▶ When you need to cut many identical pieces from the same fabric, start by cutting a strip across the width of the fabric and then subcutting the pieces. To use your fabric most efficiently, start with strips for the largest shape first. When you finish cutting the largest pieces, use the remainder of the strip for the next largest piece; then cut additional strips to fit that shape as needed. Keep cutting in the same manner until you have finished the smallest piece.

CUTTING INSTRUCTIONS FOR FOUNDATION-PIECING SEGMENTS

A pieces are used in Arc A, B pieces are used in Arc B, and so on.

A	Cut a 3″ × 3″ square. Subcut it in half on the diagonal once.
B	Cut a 3½″ × 3½″ square. Subcut it in half on the diagonal once.
C	Cut a 4″ × 4″ square. Subcut it in half on the diagonal once.
D	Cut a 2″ × 3½″ rectangle.
E	Cut a 2¼″ × 3½″ rectangle.
F	Cut a 3″ × 4″ rectangle.
G	Cut a 2¼″ × 6½″ rectangle.
H	Cut a 2½″ × 6½″ rectangle.
I	Cut a 3″ × 8½″ rectangle.

▶ Trace patterns L or M onto the wrong side of the precut fabric rectangle and cut out with scissors. Some of the pattern instructions allow you to cut strips across the width of the fabric and cut multiple L or M pieces from each strip.

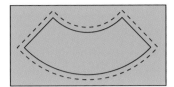

Cutting L or M pieces

▶ For pattern N, fold the precut fabric rectangle in half lengthwise (6″ × 7½″), right sides together. Align the template with the fold and trace around the template. Cut out with scissors.

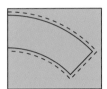

Cutting pattern N

Precutting for Template Shapes

PRECUTTING FOR BACKGROUNDS, PLAIN ARCS, AND CIRCLES

Cut a square, rectangle, or strip; then trace the pattern template and subcut each piece.

J1: Full circle	Start with a 6″ × 6″ square.
J2: Half-circle	Start with a 3½″ × 6″ rectangle.
J3: Quarter-circle	Start with a 3½″ × 3½″ square.
K: Block background	Start with a strip 4″ × width of fabric. You will be able to cut 6 K's or K-reverses from each strip.
L: Inner arc	Start with a 4″ × 8″ rectangle for 1 arc. For multiple arcs, cut a strip 8″ × width of fabric.
M: Center arc	Start with a 5″ × 11¼″ rectangle for 1 arc. For multiple arcs, cut a strip 11¼″ × width of fabric.
N: Outer arc	Start with a 6″ × 15″ rectangle for 1 arc. For multiple arcs, cut a strip 15″ × width of fabric.

Foundation Piecing

MATERIALS REQUIRED

- Foundation paper
- Fabric glue stick
- Add-A-Quarter ruler
- Index card, postcard, thin cardboard, or template plastic (to aid in using the Add-a-Quarter ruler)
- Transparent tape (to mend the foundation if you need to rip out stitches)
- Paper scissors

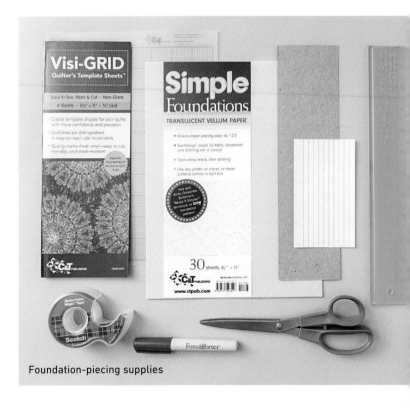

Foundation-piecing supplies

Choosing Foundation Paper

There are many choices for foundation paper in today's market—and I have tried most of them. There are specialty papers such as Carol Doak's Foundation Paper and other options such as blank newsprint-type papers. Use whatever you are comfortable with; however, I would never suggest using standard copier or printer paper. These papers are too thick and difficult to tear.

My choice of paper is vellum. I started using this paper as an instructor to make it easier for beginners to understand what was happening "behind the paper." Too many times I have heard that it is difficult to understand foundation piecing because the paper is "in the way." Vellum is semitransparent, so it is easy to place and align fabrics. You can find vellum in any art or office supply store, typically with the drafting items. Or, you can use Simple Foundations Translucent Vellum Paper (C&T Publishing).

FOUNDATION-PIECED PATTERNS

The projects in this book are based on nine different arcs, identified by letters A–I (page 84). The numbers following the letters indicate the piecing order.

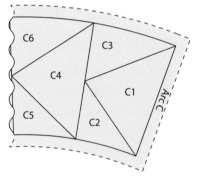

The letter indicates Arc C.

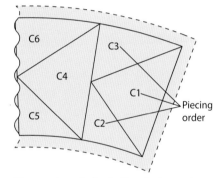

The numbers indicate the piecing order.

The solid inner lines indicate where you will sew the pieces, and the dashed outer lines show the cutting lines ¼″ past the seamlines.

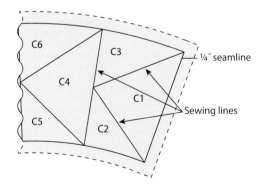

You will need to print the number of foundations indicated in the project instructions. Cut the foundations from the paper, leaving at least ¼″ of extra paper around the outer seam allowance.

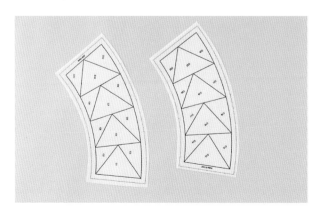

SEWING THE FOUNDATIONS

This example is based on the pattern for Arc C. Use the triangles you cut from Square C for this arc.

1. Place the first fabric right side up on the unprinted side of the foundation, centering the fabric on the C1 position and ensuring that you have adequate seam allowance around the entire piece. Use a small amount of glue to secure the fabric in place.

2. Place the foundation paper with the printed side up on your rotary cutting mat. Place the index card along the sewing line between the C1 and C2 sections and fold the foundation paper back. Place the Add-A-Quarter ruler on the foundation paper so that the lip of the ruler is pressed up against the crease and the index card. Trim the excess fabric with your rotary cutter.

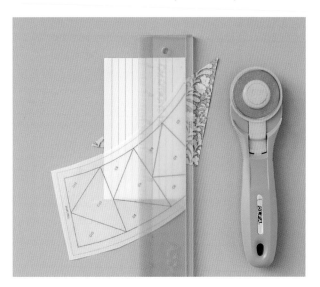

3. Fold the foundation back in place and flip it over. Place the fabric for C2, right sides together, along the edge you just trimmed on Fabric C1. Check to ensure that when you press open C2 it will completely cover the section, with adequate seam allowance on all sides.

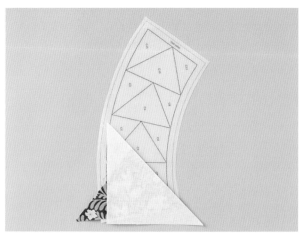

4. Hold Fabric C2 in place and flip the foundation over so that the printed side is up. Shorten your stitch length to 15–20 stitches per inch and sew on the solid line between sections C1 and C2. *Do not extend your stitching more than 1–2 stitches past the printed line.*

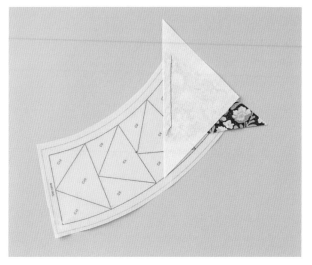

5. Trim the thread (use your machine's thread cutter if it has one) and press open Fabric C2.

> NOTE Set your iron to a low setting. Do not use steam, as this will weaken the foundation paper.

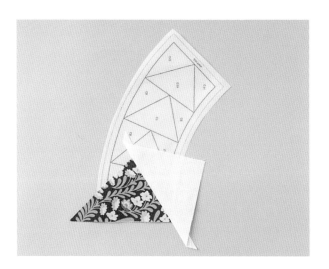

6. Place the foundation with the printed side up. Place the index card on the line between sections C1 and C3. Fold the foundation as before and use the Add-A-Quarter ruler to trim the seam allowance.

7. Place the fabric for section C3, right sides together, along the trimmed edge of Fabric C1. Once again, check to make sure that the fabric will cover the entire C3 section when pressed. Flip the foundation over and sew on the line between sections C1 and C3. Press Fabric C3 open.

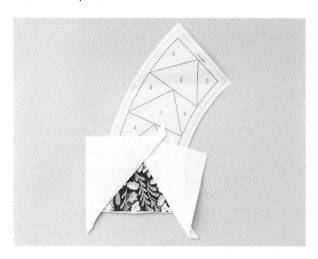

8. Continue in this manner until you have completed the entire section. Trim the foundation ¼″ from the outer solid line to be sure the pieced arc includes the seam allowance.

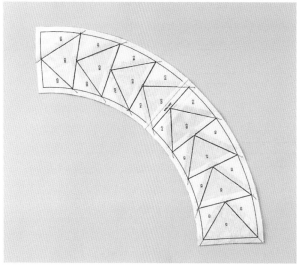

> NOTE The foundations for arcs C, F, H, and I are too large to print as a single unit on standard 8½″ × 11″ paper, so you will need to glue the halves together. Place the 2 sections so that the sewing lines overlap. Use a small amount of glue to hold the sections together and continue sewing as indicated. This is another reason I prefer vellum—I can see the lines and it is easier to position the sections.

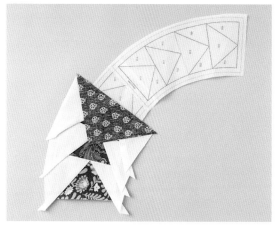

Glue the sections of large foundations together.

PIECING ORDER

It is very important to follow the piecing order, especially on the arc foundations. Arcs B, E, G, and H are sewn in the opposite direction from the arcs on either side of them so that the seams will be easy to align and match when you sew the curved foundations together.

> **NOTE: Color Placement in Reverse-Pieced Arcs**
>
> In most of the projects in this book, it will be important to place the colors in the same position in each arc. That means that when you piece arcs B, E, G, and H, you will piece the fabrics in reverse order—Fabrics 8–1, for example, instead of 1–8—in order to make the colors fall in exactly the same place in each arc.
>
> When you're asked to order fabrics in some arcs in the opposite direction, as in *Rust* (page 38) and *Crazy Tula* (page 44), pay special attention to each block's piecing order to place the fabrics in the correct position.

Curved Piecing

1. Start with the smallest section, pattern J3 (the quarter-circle) if used, and move your way out to the edge of the block.

> **NOTE** When blocks contain J1 or J2 (the full circle or half-circle), I recommend appliquéing those pieces to the pieced block. For more detailed instructions, see Appliquéd Center Circles (page 17).

Block sections to be pieced together

2. Match and pin the first 2 pieces, right sides together, at the center of each arc.

> **NOTE** When working with the plain arcs, fold them in half and gently press to mark the centers.

3. Now line up the ends and pin.

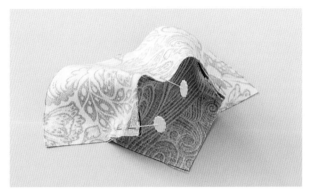

Pin the ends.

tip ▶▶▶ Use a long pin at each end and weave it in and out to securely hold the ends together and keep them from moving as you add the other pins.

4. Begin pinning between the center and corner pins, aligning the edges at the seam allowance.

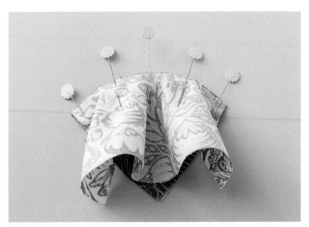

Pin around the curve.

5. Double-check to ensure that the edges are aligned and there are no big bunches or pulled areas.

6. Stitch a ¼˝ seamline, pulling the pins out just before they reach the presser foot. Watch the fabric as you stitch to be sure it doesn't shift. You may want to use a stiletto to guide the fabric under the presser foot.

7. Gently press the seam in the direction it wants to go, clipping an end to make it easier to match blocks when sewn together to form large circles.

8. Sew the remaining pieces in the same manner to complete the block.

Completed block

> NOTE When you join 2 pieced arcs, if you followed the piecing order the seam allowances will match and also be pressed in opposite directions. Abut the seams together and pin at each seamline.

Appliquéd Center Circles

You will need fusible web for this method of appliqué.

1. For a full circle, cut a J1 from the selected fabric and a J1 from fusible web.

2. Place the fabric circle on a flat surface, right side up. Lay the fusible web on top of the fabric circle with the fusible (bumpy side) down.

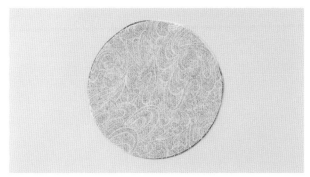

Fabric and fusible web circles

3. Stitch along the ¼″ seamline around the circle and then trim the seam allowance to ⅛″.

4. Carefully cut a slit in the fusible and flip the circle through the opening. Finger-press the seam.

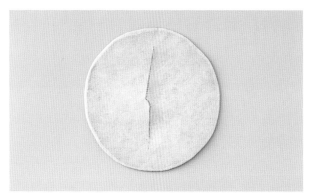

Trim the seam and turn the circle inside out.

5. Place an appliqué pressing sheet on your ironing board and lay the completed block on top, right side up. Carefully line up the circle in the center of the block, ensuring that the edge of the circle covers the ¼″ seam allowance all around the arcs. Press in place according to the instructions for your fusible web. Using a blanket or zigzag stitch, stitch the circle to the center of the block.

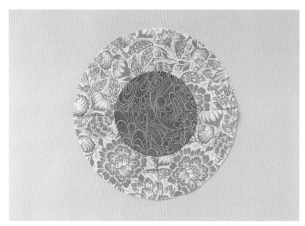

Secure the center to the block.

6. To complete the half-circles, follow Steps 1–5 using a J2 in fabric and a J2 in fusible web.

Finishing the Pillows

1. Make a block that includes 4 quarter-circles and an appliquéd J1 circle at the center.

> NOTE You will not need the K or K-reverse background pieces for these round pillows, since the K pieces are used to set a circle inside a square. Of course, if you want to make a square pillow, simply add the background pieces to the block.

2. Fold the pillow backing fabric in half, right sides together, and press lightly on the fold. Open and fold in the other direction, right sides together, and press again to mark horizontal and vertical placement lines.

3. With the fabric still folded in half, lay the pillow top on top of the backing and line up the center of the pillow with the folds. Trace around the circle. Remove the top and cut out the back with scissors.

4. Sew 2 rectangles 4½″ × 30⅜″ together end to end, with a ¼″ seam, to form a 4½″-wide ring that will go around the outside of the pillow. Pin 1 edge of this side to the pillow top, right sides together.

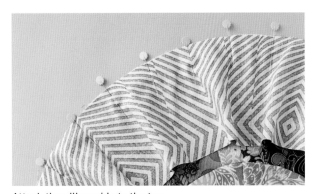

Attach the pillow side to the top.

5. Sew the pillow side to the pillow top with a ¼″ seam allowance.

6. Pin the backing to the pillow side. Leave a 4″ opening to turn and stuff the pillow.

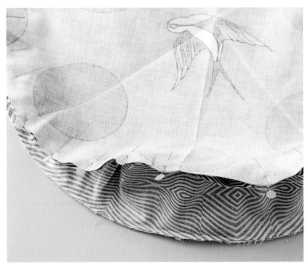

Mark the starting and stopping points with different-colored pins.

7. Sew the backing to the pillow side with a ¼″ seam, using a locking stitch at the beginning and end.

8. Turn the pillow through the opening and stuff with polyester fiberfill.

9. Hand stitch the opening closed.

The Projects

Floating Orbs

FINISHED QUILT: 100˝ × 100˝

FINISHED BLOCK (QUARTER-CIRCLE): 10˝ × 10˝

I dug into my collection of Parson Gray fabrics for this quilt. Unlike in the other quilts, in this quilt each ring of the blocks is a different color. The dark gray architectural print in the background is the perfect showcase for the vivid colors in the pieced rings and gives the eye a place to rest among all the busy color combinations. Each block is made of three colors, with the center and the outer ring in the same colorway.

Designed and made by
Carl Hentsch, quilted
by Frank Palmer, 2016

Fabrics: Prints by
Parson Gray for
FreeSpirit Fabric
and shot cottons by
Kaffe Fassett for
Westminster Fibers

MATERIALS ▶▶▶

These materials are for the quilt. To make a pillow, see Floating Orbs Pillows (page 24). Yardages are based on 42″ usable width.

This quilt consists of 3 colorways, each in 8 light fabrics and 8 dark fabrics.

ASSORTED PRINTS: 8 fat quarters for each of 6 color groupings (48 total) for pieced arcs

Group A: Dark blue

Group B: Light blue

Group C: Dark green

Group D: Light green

Group E: Dark copper/yellow

Group F: Light copper/yellow

COORDINATING SOLIDS: For pieced and plain arcs

Dark blue: 2¼ yards

Light blue: 2¼ yards

Dark green: 2¼ yards

Light green: 2¼ yards

Dark copper: 2¼ yards

Light copper: 2¼ yards

SMALL-SCALE BLACK PRINT: 2¼ yards for block backgrounds

LARGE-SCALE BLACK PRINT: 3½ yards for alternate blocks

BLACK STRIPE: ¾ yard for bias binding

BACKING: 9⅛ yards

BATTING: King-size

Foundations and patterns

Refer to Foundation-Pieced Arc Patterns (page 84) and Circle, Background, and Plain Arc Patterns (page 93). Photocopy the number of paper-piecing foundations listed. From template plastic, make templates for the circle, background, and arc patterns.

ARC A: 20

ARC B: 24

ARC C: 20

ARC D: 20

ARC E: 20

ARC F: 16

CIRCLE, BACKGROUND, AND ARC PATTERNS: J1, K, L, M, and N

CUTTING ▶▶▶

For detailed cutting instructions, refer to Cutting Pieces for the Blocks (page 11).

GROUP A

From each fat quarter:

- Cut 2 A squares, 2 B squares, and 2 C squares. Subcut each on the diagonal once.
- Cut 4 D rectangles.
- Cut 4 E rectangles.

GROUP B

From each fat quarter:

- Cut 2 A squares, 2 B squares, and 2 C squares. Subcut each on the diagonal once.
- Cut 4 E rectangles.
- Cut 4 F rectangles.

GROUP C

From each fat quarter:

- Cut 2 B squares and 2 C squares. Subcut each on the diagonal once.
- Cut 4 D rectangles
- Cut 4 E rectangles.
- Cut 4 F rectangles.

GROUP D

From each fat quarter:

- Cut 2 A squares, 2 B squares, and 2 C squares. Subcut each on the diagonal once.
- Cut 4 D rectangles.
- Cut 4 E rectangles.
- Cut 4 F rectangles.

GROUP E

From each fat quarter:

- Cut 2 A squares and 2 B squares. Subcut each on the diagonal once.
- Cut 4 D rectangles.
- Cut 4 E rectangles.

Cutting list continues ...

Cutting list continued ...

GROUP F

From each fat quarter:

- Cut 2 A squares, 2 B squares, and 2 C squares. Subcut each on the diagonal once.

- Cut 4 D rectangles.

- Cut 4 F rectangles.

DARK BLUE SOLID

- Cut 32 A squares, 32 B squares, and 32 C squares. Subcut each on the diagonal once.

- Cut 4 L arcs.

- Cut 4 N arcs.

- Cut 3 J1 circles.

LIGHT BLUE SOLID

- Cut 32 A squares, 32 B squares, and 32 C squares. Subcut each on the diagonal once.

- Cut 4 M arcs.

- Cut 1 J1 circle.

DARK GREEN SOLID

- Cut 32 B squares and 32 C squares. Subcut each on the diagonal once.

- Cut 2 J1 circles.

LIGHT GREEN SOLID

- Cut 32 A squares, 32 B squares, and 32 C squares. Subcut each on the diagonal once.

- Cut 4 L arcs.

- Cut 4 N arcs.

- Cut 3 J1 circles.

DARK COPPER SOLID

- Cut 32 A squares and 32 B squares. Subcut each on the diagonal once.

- Cut 4 L arcs.

- Cut 4 M arcs.

- Cut 4 N arcs.

- Cut 3 J1 circles.

LIGHT COPPER SOLID

- Cut 32 A squares, 32 B squares, and 32 C squares. Subcut each on the diagonal once.

- Cut 4 N arcs.

- Cut 1 J1 circle.

SMALL-SCALE BLACK PRINT

- Cut 52 K and 52 K-reverse backgrounds.

LARGE-SCALE BLACK PRINT

- Cut 12 squares 20½″ × 20½″.

BINDING

- Cut enough 2¼″ bias binding strips to make 410″ of bias binding.

BACKING

- Cut 3 pieces 108″ × width of fabric.

Quilt Construction

To see how the blocks are assembled, refer to Block Index (page 76). For foundation- and curved-piecing and appliqué techniques, refer to Making the Blocks (page 10).

1. Arrange the assorted prints in a row within each group, with each fabric color flowing into the next. Choose the first fabric and label it Fabric 1. Working from left to right, label the rest of the fabrics 2–8.

2. Match the fabric pieces by letter with the foundations for the arcs. Using the foundations listed in Foundations and Patterns (page 21), foundation piece the arcs in sets of 4 arcs each. Use the colors in exactly the same positions in all the arcs.

3. Combine the pieced arcs with the L, M, and N plain arcs and the K and K-reverse backgrounds to make 4 matching quarter-blocks for each of Blocks 01, 02, 03, 05, 10, 11, 16, 17, 18, 21, 25, 29, and 30. Do not add the circle piece yet.

4. Sew the matching quarter-circles together to make 13 full-circle blocks. To finish each large block, appliqué a J1 circle to the center.

5. Referring to the quilt assembly diagram, arrange the blocks in rows, with plain blocks between the pieced blocks. Sew the blocks in each row together.

6. Sew the rows together to complete the quilt top.

Finishing the Quilt

Sew the backing sections together and trim to make a 108″ × 108″ square for the backing. Layer, quilt, and bind as desired. Frank Palmer quilted a beautiful feather pattern in the plain arcs on my quilt. In the big alternate squares, he stitched a complex set of parallel lines.

Quilt assembly

Floating Orbs
PILLOWS

COORDINATING PILLOWS: 19˝ diameter × 4˝

 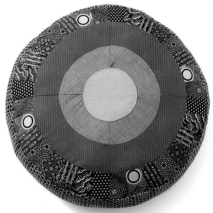 

MATERIALS

If you are making the quilt, you will have enough leftover fabric to make at least 1 pillow top. To make all 5 pillows, you will need the following:

ASSORTED PRINTS: 8 fat eighths for each of 5 color groupings (40 total) for pieced arcs

GROUP A: Dark blue

GROUP B: Light blue

GROUP C: Dark green

GROUP D: Dark copper/yellow

GROUP E: Light copper/yellow

COORDINATING SOLIDS: For Flying Geese backgrounds and plain arcs

DARK BLUE SOLID: ⅜ yard

LIGHT BLUE SOLID: ¾ yard

DARK GREEN SOLID: 1¼ yards

LIGHT GREEN SOLID: ⅜ yard

DARK COPPER SOLID: ⅞ yard

LIGHT COPPER SOLID: ⅜ yard

SMALL-SCALE BLACK PRINT: 1⅜ yards for pillow sides

LARGE-SCALE BLACK PRINT: 1¾ yards for pillow backs

POLYESTER FIBERFILL: 5 pounds

Foundations and patterns

Refer to Foundation-Pieced Arc Patterns (page 84) and Circle, Background, and Plain Arc Patterns (page 93). Photocopy the number of paper-piecing foundations listed. From template plastic, make templates for the circle and arc patterns.

ARC A: 4

ARC C: 4

ARC D: 4

ARC E: 4

ARC F: 8

CIRCLE AND ARC PATTERNS: J1, L, M, and N

CUTTING

For detailed cutting instructions, refer to Cutting Pieces for the Blocks (page 11).

GROUP A
- From each fat eighth, cut 4 F rectangles.

GROUP B
- From each fat eighth, cut 4 D rectangles.

GROUP C
- From each fat eighth, cut 2 A squares. Subcut each on the diagonal once.

GROUP D
From each fat eighth:
- Cut 2 C squares. Subcut each on the diagonal once.
- Cut 4 F rectangles.

GROUP E
- From each fat eighth, cut 4 E rectangles.

DARK BLUE SOLID
- Cut 4 M arcs.

LIGHT BLUE SOLID
- Cut 4 L arcs.
- Cut 4 N arcs.
- Cut 2 J1 circles.

DARK GREEN SOLID
- Cut 32 A squares. Subcut each on the diagonal once.
- Cut 4 L arcs.
- Cut 4 M arcs.
- Cut 4 N arcs.
- Cut 1 J1 circle.

LIGHT GREEN SOLID
- Cut 4 M arcs.

DARK COPPER SOLID
- Cut 32 C squares. Subcut each on the diagonal once.
- Cut 4 L arcs.
- Cut 2 J1 circles.

LIGHT COPPER SOLID
- Cut 4 M arcs.

SMALL-SCALE BLACK PRINT
- Cut 10 rectangles 4½″ × 30⅜″.

LARGE-SCALE BLACK PRINT
- Cut 5 squares 21″ × 21″.

Pillow Construction

1. Using the techniques in Quilt Construction, Steps 1–3 (page 22), sew any combination of inner, center, and outer arcs together to complete 4 quarter-circles for each pillow. To make the round pillows, do not add the K background pieces.

2. Refer to Finishing the Pillows (page 18) to learn how to assemble the pillows.

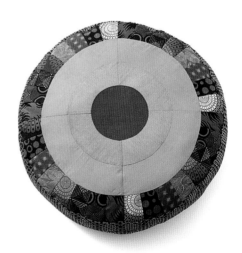

Pandemonium

JEWELS OF THE AMAZON

FINISHED QUILT: 80˝ × 80˝

FINISHED BLOCK (QUARTER-CIRCLE): 10˝ × 10˝

Webster's defines *pandemonium* as "a wild uproar," which fits to describe being around a flock of wild parrots. This quilt was inspired by the lush tropics of the Amazon rain forest and the brightly colored parrots flying high in the treetops.

The fabric selection for this quilt began with a fat-quarter bundle of Kaffe Fassett shot cottons. The large floral print and three background fabrics coordinate perfectly with the 32 fat quarters.

Designed and made by Carl Hentsch, quilted by Teresa Silva, 2015

Fabrics: Shot cottons and Kaffe Classics by Kaffe Fassett for Westminster Fibers

MATERIALS ▸▸▸

These materials are for the quilt. To make a pillow, see Pandemonium Pillows (page 30). Yardages are based on 42˝ usable width.

ASSORTED SOLIDS: 32 fat quarters for pieced arcs

POLKA-DOT PRINT: 1⅜ yards for pieced arc backgrounds and plain inner arcs

SMALL-SCALE PRINT: 3 yards for pieced arc backgrounds and plain center arcs

MEDIUM-SCALE PRINT: 2⅞ yards for pieced arc backgrounds and plain outer arcs

LARGE-SCALE FLORAL PRINT: 3¼ yards for block backgrounds, circles, and half-circles

MULTICOLOR STRIPE: ⅝ yard for bias binding

BACKING: 7⅜ yards

BATTING: Queen-size

Foundations and patterns

Refer to Foundation-Pieced Arc Patterns (page 84) and Circle, Background, and Plain Arc Patterns (page 93). Photocopy the number of paper-piecing foundations listed. From template plastic, make templates for the circle, background, and arc patterns.

ARC A: 16	ARC E: 16
ARC B: 32	ARC F: 32
ARC C: 16	CIRCLE, BACKGROUND,
ARC D: 32	AND ARC PATTERNS:
	J1, J2, K, L, M, and N

CUTTING ▸▸▸

For detailed cutting instructions, refer to Cutting Pieces for the Blocks (page 11).

ASSORTED SOLIDS
From each fat quarter:

- Cut 2 A squares, 4 B squares, and 2 C squares. Subcut each on the diagonal once.
- Cut 8 D rectangles.
- Cut 4 E rectangles.
- Cut 8 F rectangles.

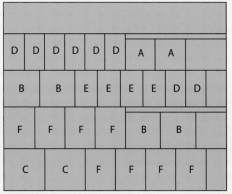

Fat quarter cutting diagram

POLKA-DOT PRINT

- Cut 16 L arcs.
- Cut 128 A squares. Subcut each on the diagonal once.

SMALL-SCALE PRINT

- Cut 16 M arcs.
- Cut 256 B squares. Subcut each on the diagonal once.

MEDIUM-SCALE PRINT

- Cut 16 N arcs.
- Cut 128 C squares. Subcut each on the diagonal once.

LARGE-SCALE FLORAL PRINT

- Cut 64 K and 64 K-reverse backgrounds.
- Fussy cut 14 J1 circles and 4 J2 half-circles.

BINDING

- Cut enough 2¼˝ bias strips to make 330˝ of bias binding.

BACKING

- Cut 3 pieces 88˝ × width of fabric.

Quilt Construction

To see how the blocks are assembled, refer to Block Index (page 76). For foundation- and curved-piecing techniques, refer to Making the Blocks (page 10).

1. Keeping the assorted prints in their general color groups, arrange the fabrics for each group in a circle, with each fabric color flowing into the next. Choose a fabric anywhere in the circle and label it Fabric 1. Working clockwise around the circle, label the rest of the fabrics 2–32.

2. Match the fabric pieces by letter with the printed foundations for the arcs. Foundation piece the arcs listed in Foundations and Patterns (page 27) in sets of 4 arcs each. Use the fabrics in a single color group to complete all 4 arcs, which you should label quadrants A, B, C, and D. Start with Fabric 1; use Fabrics 1–8 for quadrant A, Fabrics 9–16 for quadrant B, and so on. Use the fabrics in exactly the same positions in all the sets of arcs.

3. Combine the pieced arcs with the L, M, and N plain arcs and the K and K-reverse backgrounds to make 4 sets of quarter-blocks from each of Blocks 05, 17, 22, and 25. Do not add the center-circle pieces yet.

4. Sew the quarter-blocks within each color group together to make 4 full-circle blocks each for Blocks 17 and 22. Make 3 full-circle blocks and 2 half-blocks each for Blocks 05 and 25.

5. To finish each block, appliqué a J1 circle to the full-circle blocks or a J2 half-circle to the half-circle blocks.

6. Referring to the quilt assembly diagram (next page), arrange the blocks in rows. In each row, rotate each successive full-circle block a quarter-turn so a different part of the color wheel is at the top of the block. Sew the blocks in each row together.

7. Sew the rows together to complete the quilt top.

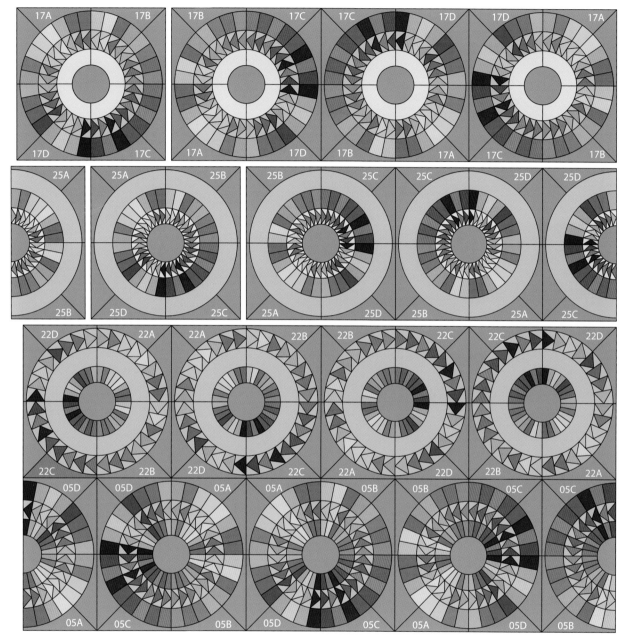

Quilt assembly

Finishing the Quilt

Sew the backing sections together to make an 88″ × 86″ piece for the backing. Layer, quilt, and bind as desired. Teresa Silva quilted a swirly petal pattern in some of the plain arcs in this quilt, giving the large circles a bit of a floral look.

Pandemonium
PILLOWS

COORDINATING PILLOWS: 19˝ diameter × 4˝

MATERIALS ▸▸▸

If you are making the quilt, you will have enough leftover fabric to make at least 1 pillow top. For 3 pillows you will need the following:

ASSORTED SOLIDS:
32 squares 10˝ × 10˝

POLKA-DOT PRINT: ⅝ yard

SMALL-SCALE PRINT: ¾ yard

MEDIUM-SCALE PRINT: 1 yard

LARGE-SCALE FLORAL PRINT:
1 yard for pillow sides

BACKING: 1¼ yards

POLYESTER FIBERFILL:
3 pounds

Foundations and patterns

Refer to Foundation-Pieced Arc Patterns (page 84) and Circle, Background, and Plain Arc Patterns (page 93). Photocopy the number of paper-piecing foundations listed. From template plastic, make templates for the circle and arc patterns.

ARC A: 4

ARC B: 4

ARC C: 4

ARC D: 4

ARC E: 4

ARC F: 4

CIRCLE AND ARC PATTERNS:
J1, L, M, and N

CUTTING ▸▸▸

For detailed cutting instructions, refer to Cutting Pieces for the Blocks (page 11).

ASSORTED SOLIDS

From each 10″ square:

- Cut 1 A square, 1 B square, and 1 C square. Subcut each on the diagonal once.
- Cut 1 D rectangle.
- Cut 1 E rectangle.
- Cut 1 F rectangle.

POLKA-DOT PRINT

- Cut 4 L arcs.
- Cut 32 A squares. Subcut each on the diagonal once.

SMALL-SCALE PRINT

- Cut 4 M arcs.
- Cut 32 B squares. Subcut each on the diagonal once.

MEDIUM-SCALE PRINT

- Cut 4 N arcs.
- Cut 32 C squares. Subcut each on the diagonal once.

LARGE-SCALE FLORAL PRINT

- Cut 6 rectangles 4½″ × 30⅜″.
- Fussy cut 3 J1 circles.

BACKING

- Cut 3 squares 21″ × 21″.

Pillow Construction

1. Using the techniques in Quilt Construction, Steps 1–3 (page 28), sew pieced and plain arcs together to complete 4 each of Blocks 17, 22, and 25. To make the round pillows, do not add the K background pieces.

2. Refer to Finishing the Pillows (page 18) to learn how to assemble the pillows.

Twin Dragons
THE LEGEND OF YIN AND YANG

FINISHED QUILT: 60″ × 70″

FINISHED BLOCK (QUARTER-CIRCLE): 10″ × 10″

Designed and made by Carl Hentsch, quilted by Teresa Silva, 2015

Fabrics: Prints by Carolyn Friedlander for Robert Kaufman Fabrics and Pure Elements Solids by Art Gallery Fabrics

This quilt tells the story of the Twin Dragons. An emperor's twin children, Yin and Yang, ate fruit from the garden of an evil witch, who placed a curse on them. Yin became Dragon of the Sky, forever circling the earth. Her moving wings caused wild storms; her icy cold breath made snow fall. Yang became Dragon of the Earth, living underground. His movements made the earth tremble, and his fiery breath caused volcanoes to erupt.

With the organic movement in this quilt, I knew that I wanted the Flying Geese units to ground the quilt and emphasize the movement and direction of the design. We chose a solid for those areas. We started with two fat-quarter bundles, easily separated into the two colorways of turquoise/blue and yellow/orange. Then I picked navy and black for the solids and background sections. Small-scale prints worked against the solids in the Flying Geese arcs.

MATERIALS ▶▶▶

These materials are for the quilt. To make a pillow, see Yin and Yang Pillows (page 36). Yardages are based on 42˝ usable width.

This quilt is made from 2 colorways. The quilt is a mirror image, so you will need to make a block in each colorway.

COLORWAY 1, BLUE

Assorted blue prints: 8 fat quarters, light blue to dark blue, for pieced arcs

Navy blue solid: 1 yard for pieced arcs

Small-scale print 1: ¾ yard for plain arcs

Medium-scale print 1: 1¼ yards for plain arcs

Large-scale print 1: 1⅔ yards for plain arcs

Navy print: 1¼ yards for block background

COLORWAY 2, GOLD

Assorted gold prints: 8 fat quarters, yellow to dark gold

Black solid: 1 yard for pieced arcs

Small-scale print 2: ¾ yard for plain arcs

Medium-scale print 2: 1¼ yards for plain arcs

Large-scale print 2: 1⅔ yards for plain arcs

Black print: 1¼ yards for block background

OTHER

Backing: 3⅞ yards

Cream-and-black stripe: ½ yard for bias binding

Batting: Full/double-size

Foundations and patterns

Refer to Foundation-Pieced Arc Patterns (page 84) and Circle, Background, and Plain Arc Patterns (page 93). Photocopy the number of paper-piecing foundations listed. From template plastic, make templates for the circle, background, and arc patterns.

ARC A: 14	ARC E: 8	CIRCLE, BACK-
ARC B: 18	ARC F: 12	GROUND, AND
ARC C: 16	ARC G: 2	ARC PATTERNS:
ARC D: 10	ARC I: 2	J3, K, L, M, and N

CUTTING ▶▶▶

For detailed cutting instructions, refer to Cutting Pieces for the Blocks (page 11).

Cut the same pieces from both colorways.

ASSORTED PRINTS

From each fat quarter in both colorways:

- Cut 5 D rectangles.
- Cut 4 E rectangles.
- Cut 6 F rectangles.
- Cut 1 G rectangle.
- Cut 1 I rectangle.

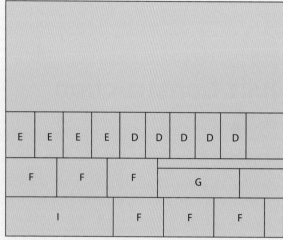

Fat quarter cutting diagram for blues and golds

NAVY BLUE SOLID AND BLACK SOLID

- From each solid, cut 28 A squares, 36 B squares, and 32 C squares. Subcut each on the diagonal once.

SMALL-SCALE PRINTS 1 AND 2

From each print:

- Cut 7 L arcs.
- Cut 56 A squares. Subcut each on the diagonal once.

MEDIUM-SCALE PRINTS 1 AND 2

From each print:

- Cut 6 M arcs.
- Cut 72 B squares. Subcut each on the diagonal once.

Cutting list continues …

Cutting list continued ...

LARGE-SCALE PRINTS 1 AND 2

From each print:

- Cut 6 N arcs.

- Cut 64 C squares. Subcut each on the diagonal once.

NAVY PRINT AND BLACK PRINT

From each print:

- Cut 21 K and 21 K-reverse backgrounds.

- Cut 21 J3 quarter-circles.

BINDING

- Cut enough bias strips 2¼″ × width of fabric to make 270″ of bias binding.

BACKING

- Cut 2 pieces 68″ × width of fabric.

Quilt Construction

To see how the blocks are assembled, refer to Block Index (page 76). For foundation- and curved-piecing techniques, refer to Making the Blocks (page 10).

1. Keeping the assorted prints in their general color groups, arrange the fabrics in a row, starting with the lightest fabric and gradating to the darkest. Label the fabrics 1–8.

2. Match the fabric pieces by letter with the printed foundations for the arcs. Foundation piece each of the arcs listed in Foundations and Patterns (page 33). Use the colors in exactly the same positions in all the arcs.

3. Combine the pieced arcs with the J3 quarter-circles; L, M, and N plain arcs; and K and K-reverse backgrounds to complete 1 each of Blocks 01, 02, 03, 04, 05, 06, 08, 09, 11, 12, 13, 14, 16, 17, 18, 20, 21, 22, 24, 25, and 31 in each colorway.

4. Referring to the quilt assembly diagram (next page), arrange the blocks in rows. Sew the blocks in each row together.

5. Sew the rows together to complete the quilt top.

Quilt assembly

Finishing the Quilt

Sew the backing sections together to make a 68″ × 78″ rectangle.
Layer, quilt, and bind as desired. Teresa Silva quilted a large echoed
swirly line through some of the arcs and a tighter interlocking
figure-eight pattern through other arcs.

Yin and Yang
PILLOWS

COORDINATING PILLOWS: 19˝ diameter × 4˝

MATERIALS ▸▸▸

If you are making the quilt, you will be able to use leftover fabric instead of buying the fat eighths. For 2 pillows you will need the following:

COLORWAY 1, BLUE

Assorted prints: 8 fat eighths, light blue to dark blue

Navy blue solid: ⅓ yard

Small-scale print 1: ¼ yard

Medium-scale print 1: ½ yard

Large-scale print: ⅓ yard

Navy print: ½ yard for pillow sides and center circle

COLORWAY 2, GOLD

Assorted prints: 8 fat eighths, yellow to dark gold

Black solid: ⅓ yard

Small-scale print 2: ½ yard

Medium-scale print 2: ⅝ yard

Large-scale print 2: ⅓ yard

Black print: ½ yard for pillow sides and center circle

OTHER

Backing: ⅝ yard

Polyester fiberfill: 2 pounds

Foundations and patterns

Refer to Foundation-Pieced Arc Patterns (page 84) and Circle, Background, and Plain Arc Patterns (page 93). Photocopy the number of paper-piecing foundations listed. From template plastic, make templates for the circle and arc patterns.

ARC A: 2	ARC E: 1
ARC B: 3	ARC F: 4
ARC C: 4	ARC G: 1
ARC D: 3	CIRCLE AND ARC PATTERNS: J1, L, and M

CUTTING ▶▶▶

For detailed cutting instructions, refer to Cutting Pieces for the Blocks (page 11).

COLORWAY 1, BLUE

Assorted prints

From each fat eighth:

- Cut 2 D rectangles.
- Cut 2 F rectangles.
- Cut 1 G rectangle.

Navy blue solid

- Cut 4 A squares, 8 B squares, and 8 C squares. Subcut each on the diagonal once.

Small-scale print 1

- Cut 8 A squares. Subcut each on the diagonal once.

Medium-scale print 1

- Cut 1 M arc.
- Cut 16 B squares. Subcut each on the diagonal once.

Large-scale print 1

- Cut 16 C squares. Subcut each on the diagonal once.

Navy print

- Cut 2 rectangles 4½″ × 30⅜″.
- Fussy cut 1 J1 circle.

COLORWAY 2, GOLD

Assorted prints

From each fat eighth:

- Cut 1 D rectangle.
- Cut 1 E rectangle.
- Cut 2 F rectangles.

Black solid

- Cut 4 A squares, 4 B squares, and 8 C squares. Subcut each on the diagonal once.

Small-scale print 2

- Cut 2 L arcs.
- Cut 8 A squares. Subcut each on the diagonal once.

Medium-scale print 2

- Cut 2 M arcs.
- Cut 8 B squares. Subcut each on the diagonal once.

Large-scale print 2

- Cut 16 C squares. Subcut each on the diagonal once.

Black print

- Cut 2 rectangles 4½″ × 30⅜″.
- Fussy cut 1 J1 circle.

BACKING

- Cut 2 squares 21″ × 21″.

Pillow Construction

1. Using the techniques in Quilt Construction, Steps 1–3 (page 34), sew pieced and plain arcs together to complete 1 quarter-circle for each Block 04, 05, 06, and 22 in the blue colorway and 1 for each Block 17, 21, 22, and 24 in the gold colorway. To make the round pillows, do not add the K background pieces.

2. Refer to Finishing the Pillows (page 18) to learn how to assemble the pillows.

Rust

WHEN SALT WATER MEETS COTTON AND STEEL

FINISHED QUILT: 60″ × 60″

FINISHED BLOCK (QUARTER-CIRCLE): 10″ × 10″

This quilt was inspired by the traditional Clamshell quilt. It is a modern twist, with large pieced blocks and modern fabrics.

The color for this quilt was inspired by the three colorways of the Salt Water fabric line by Tula Pink.

I had to dig deep in my stash to recover these fabrics. I paired those colors with the Basics collection from Cotton + Steel, which blended perfectly with them. I added shot cottons to the Flying Geese arcs. The centers are half-circles fussy cut from a larger-scale print.

Designed and made by Carl Hentsch, quilted by Angela Walters, 2016

Fabrics: Salt Water by Tula Pink for FreeSpirit Fabric, Kaffe Fassett shot cottons for Westminster Fibers, and Cotton + Steel Basics by RJR Fabrics

MATERIALS ▸▸▸

These materials are for the quilt. To make a pillow, see Rust Pillows (page 42). Yardages are based on 42˝ usable width.

This quilt consists of 3 colorways (blue, green, and orange). For each colorway you will need the following:

ASSORTED SMALL-SCALE PRINTS: 8 fat quarters for pieced arcs

SOLID: ⅞ yard for Flying Geese backgrounds

TONE-ON-TONE PRINT: ⅝ yard for plain inner arcs

LARGE-SCALE PRINT: 1 yard for block backgrounds and center half-circles

MULTICOLOR STRIPE: ½ yard for bias binding

BACKING: 3⅞ yards

BATTING: Twin-size

Foundations and patterns

Refer to Foundation-Pieced Arc Patterns (page 84) and Circle, Background, and Plain Arc Patterns (page 93). Photocopy the number of paper-piecing foundations listed. From template plastic, make templates for the circle, background, and arc patterns.

ARC B: 36

ARC F: 36

CIRCLE, BACKGROUND, AND ARC PATTERNS: J2, J3, K, and L

CUTTING ▸▸▸

For detailed cutting instructions, refer to Cutting Pieces for the Blocks (page 11).

FROM EACH OF THE 3 COLORWAYS

Assorted small-scale prints
From each fat quarter:

• Cut 6 B squares. Subcut each on the diagonal once.

• Cut 12 F rectangles.

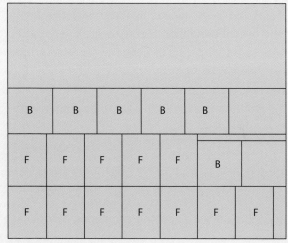

Fat quarter cutting diagram

Solid

• Cut 96 B squares. Subcut each on the diagonal once.

Tone-on-tone print

• Cut 12 L arcs.

Large-scale print

• Cut 12 K and 12 K-reverse arcs.

• Fussy cut 5 J2 half-circles and 2 J3 quarter-circles.

BINDING

• Cut enough 2¼˝ bias strips to make 250˝ of bias binding.

BACKING

• Cut 2 pieces 68˝ × width of fabric.

Quilt Construction

To see how the blocks are assembled, refer to Block Index (page 76). For foundation- and curved-piecing techniques, refer to Making the Blocks (page 10).

1. Keeping the assorted small-scale prints in their general color groups, arrange the fabrics for each group in an arc, with each fabric color flowing into the next. Label the fabrics from left to right, 1–8.

2. Match the fabric pieces by letter with the printed foundations for the arcs. Foundation piece the arcs listed in Foundations and Patterns (page 39) in 2 sets of 6 per color group. In each group, piece 6 of the arcs starting with Fabric 1; piece the other 6, starting with Fabric 8 and adding the colors in reverse order. Use the colors in exactly the same positions in all the arcs.

3. Combine the pieced arcs with plain arc L and backgrounds K and K-reverse to make 12 of Block 17 in *each* colorway. In 2 blocks in each colorway, add the J3 quarter-circle to complete the block. Wait to add the centers to the remaining blocks.

4. In each colorway, sew the remaining blocks together to make 5 mirrored pairs. To finish each pair, appliqué a J2 half-circle to the center of the block.

5. Referring to the quilt assembly diagram (next page), arrange the blocks in rows. Sew the blocks in each row together.

6. Sew the rows together to complete the quilt top.

Finishing the Quilt

Sew the backing sections together to make a 68″ × 68″ square. Layer, quilt, and bind as desired. Quilter Angela Walters created a different quilting pattern for each colorway in the quilt. The patterns add a little contrast between the color sections, yet a similarity of scale keeps them from looking too different. For fun, she outlined the octopus in each center half-circle.

Quilt assembly

Rust
PILLOWS

COORDINATING PILLOWS: 19˝ diameter × 4˝

MATERIALS ▸▸▸

If you are making the quilt, you will be able to use leftover fabric instead of buying the 10˝ squares. To make the 3 pillows, you will need the following in each of the 3 colorways:

ASSORTED SMALL-SCALE PRINTS:
8 squares 10˝ × 10˝

SOLID: ½ yard

TONE-ON-TONE PRINT: ⅜ yard

LARGE-SCALE PRINT: ⅜ yard for pillow sides and center circles

BACKING: ⅝ yard

POLYESTER FIBERFILL: 1 pound per pillow

Foundations and patterns

Refer to Foundation-Pieced Arc Patterns (page 84) and Circle, Background, and Plain Arc Patterns (page 93). Photocopy the number of paper-piecing foundations listed. From template plastic, make templates for the circle and arc patterns.

ARC B: 12

ARC F: 12

CIRCLE AND ARC PATTERNS: J1 or J2 and L

CUTTING

For detailed cutting instructions, refer to Cutting Pieces for the Blocks (page 11).

FROM EACH OF THE 3 COLORWAYS

Assorted small-scale prints

From each 10″ square:

- Cut 2 B squares. Subcut each on the diagonal once.

- Cut 4 F rectangles.

Solid

- Cut 32 B squares. Subcut each on the diagonal once.

Tone-on-tone print

- Cut 4 L arcs.

Large-scale print

- Cut 2 rectangles 4½″ × 30⅜″.

- Cut 1 J1 circle or 1 matching pair of J2 half-circles. (I used mirror images of half-circles for my pillows.)

BACKING

- Cut 1 square 21″ × 21″.

Pillow Construction

1. Using the techniques in Quilt Construction, Steps 1–3 (page 40), sew the arcs together to complete 4 quarter-circles from Block 17 in any colorway to make 1 pillow, or you can make 4 quarter-circles in each colorway to make all 3 pillows. For each pillow, make 2 quadrants with the fabrics in order 1–8. Reverse the order in the remaining 2 quadrants. To make the round pillows, do not add the K background pieces.

2. Refer to Finishing the Pillows (page 18) to learn how to assemble the pillows.

Crazy Tula

FINISHED QUILT: 60″ × 60″

FINISHED BLOCK (QUARTER CIRCLE): 10″ × 10″

I loved having the support and encouragement of my friend Tula Pink on this project. For this quilt, I gave Tula a blank canvas—the quilt layout with plain blocks, requesting to "go crazy" and select fabrics and determine their placements in the blocks. This was an awesome collaboration with Tula's color sense and my complex quilt designs.

This quilt is slightly different from most of the other quilts in the book, as some of the arcs have the colors pieced in reverse order. For the block backgrounds, we pulled multiple prints from the same fabrics I used in the plain arcs. For some of the plain arcs, we chose two cream tones to help separate the pieced arcs.

Designed and made by Carl Hentsch, quilted by Angela Walters, 2016

Fabrics: Various prints by Tula Pink for FreeSpirit Fabric, FreeSpirit Designer Essentials Solids, and Essex Linen by Robert Kaufman

MATERIALS ▸▸▸

These materials are for the quilt. To make a pillow, see Crazy Tula Pillows (page 48). Yardages are based on 42″ usable width.

ASSORTED FOCUS PRINTS: 24 fat quarters ranging from red to purple (3 reds, 3 pinks, 2 oranges, 3 yellows, 4 greens, 4 blues, and 5 purples) for pieced arcs (Choose shades that blend nicely from color to color.)

COORDINATING PRINTS: for plain arcs and block backgrounds

Red print: ¼ yard	**Green print 3:** ¼ yard
Pink print 1: ¼ yard	**Blue print 1:** ¼ yard
Pink print 2: ¼ yard	**Blue print 2:** ¼ yard
Yellow print 1: ¼ yard	**Blue print 3:** ¼ yard
Yellow print 2: ¼ yard	**Purple print 1:** ¼ yard
Yellow print 3: ¼ yard	**Purple print 2:** ¼ yard
Green print 1: ¼ yard	**Purple print 3:** ¼ yard
Green print 2: ¼ yard	

CREAM SOLID: 2 yards for Flying Geese backgrounds, plain arcs, quarter-circles, and backgrounds

LINEN SOLID: 2½ yards for Flying Geese backgrounds, plain arcs, quarter-circles, and backgrounds

MULTICOLOR FLORAL: ¾ yard for binding

BACKING: 5 yards (includes pillow backs)

BATTING: Twin-size

Foundations and patterns

Refer to Foundation-Pieced Arc Patterns (page 84) and Circle, Background, and Plain Arc Patterns (page 93). Photocopy the number of paper-piecing foundations listed. From template plastic, make templates for the circle, background, and arc patterns.

ARC B: 6	ARC F: 9	CIRCLE, BACKGROUND, AND ARC PATTERNS: J3, K, L, M, and N
ARC C: 12	ARC G: 6	
ARC D: 15	ARC I: 3	
ARC E: 15		

CUTTING ▸▸▸

For detailed cutting instructions, refer to Cutting Pieces for the Blocks (page 11). Before you start cutting, arrange the prints in order, with each color flowing into the next, and label them 1–24.

ASSORTED FOCUS PRINTS

From each fat quarter:

- Cut 1 B square and 2 C squares. Subcut each on the diagonal once.
- Cut 5 D rectangles.
- Cut 5 E rectangles.
- Cut 3 F rectangles.
- Cut 2 G rectangles.
- Cut 1 I rectangle.

From 1 red fat quarter:

- Cut 2 J3 quarter-circles.

COORDINATING PRINTS

Red print
- Cut 3 K and 3 K-reverse backgrounds.

Pink print 1
- Cut 3 K and 3 K-reverse backgrounds.

Pink print 2
- Cut 2 K and 2 K-reverse backgrounds.
- Cut 1 J3 quarter-circle.

Yellow print 1
- Cut 2 K and 2 K-reverse backgrounds.
- Cut 1 J3 quarter-circle.

Yellow print 2
- Cut 1 L arc.

Yellow print 3
- Cut 1 N arc.
- Cut 3 J3 quarter-circles.

Green print 1
- Cut 2 K and 2 K-reverse backgrounds.
- Cut 3 J3 quarter-circles.

Green print 2
- Cut 3 K and 3 K-reverse backgrounds.
- Cut 1 L arc.
- Cut 2 J3 quarter-circles.

Cutting list continues ...

Cutting list continued …

COORDINATING PRINTS

Green print 3

- Cut 3 K and 3 K-reverse backgrounds.
- Cut 1 J3 quarter-circle.

Blue print 1

- Cut 1 K and 1 K-reverse backgrounds.
- Cut 3 L arcs.

Blue print 2

- Cut 3 K and 3 K-reverse backgrounds.

Blue print 3

- Cut 3 K and 3 K-reverse backgrounds.

Purple print 1

- Cut 2 K and 2 K-reverse backgrounds.

Purple print 2

- Cut 2 L arcs.

Purple print 3

- Cut 2 J3 quarter-circles.

CREAM SOLID

- Cut 5 N arcs.
- Cut 6 M arcs.
- Cut 6 K and 6 K-reverse backgrounds.
- Cut 24 C squares. Subcut each on the diagonal once.
- Cut 9 J3 quarter-circles.

LINEN SOLID

- Cut 6 N arcs.
- Cut 5 L arcs.
- Cut 3 K and 3 K-reverse backgrounds.
- Cut 48 B squares and 72 C squares. Subcut each on the diagonal once.
- Cut 9 J3 quarter-circles.

BINDING

- Cut 7 strips 2¼″ × width of fabric to make 250″ of binding.

BACKING

- Cut 2 pieces 68″ × width of fabric.

Quilt Construction

To see how the blocks are assembled, refer to Block Index (page 84). For foundation- and curved-piecing techniques, refer to Making the Blocks (page 10).

1. Divide the assorted focus fabrics into general color groups and then arrange the fabrics in an arc, with each fabric color flowing into the next. Choose the first fabric and label it Fabric 1. Working clockwise around the arc, label the rest of the fabrics 2–24.

2. Match the fabric pieces by letter with the printed foundations for the arcs. Foundation piece the arcs listed in Foundations and Patterns (page 45) in sets of 3 arcs each, which you should label quadrants A, B, and C. In most cases, start with Fabric 1 and use Fabrics 1–8 for quadrant A, Fabrics 9–16 for quadrant B, and Fabrics 17–24 for quadrant C. Use the fabrics in exactly the same positions in all the sets of arcs.

3. In some arcs, the color sequence should be arranged in the opposite direction. Use Fabrics 8–1 for quadrant A, Fabrics 16–9 for quadrant B, and so on. See the chart below.

COLOR PLACEMENT FOR ARCS

Fabric order	Arc B	Arc C	Arc D	Arc E	Arc F	Arc G	Arc I
1–8	2	3	1	1	2	1	1
8–1	0	1	4	4	1	1	0
9–16	1	3	2	1	3	1	1
16–9	1	1	3	4	0	1	0
17–24	1	3	2	1	3	1	1
24–17	1	1	3	4	0	1	0

4. Still working in sets of 3, combine the pieced arcs with matching J3 quarter-circles; plain arcs L, M, and N; and the K and K-reverse backgrounds to make the following blocks:

- ▶ Blocks 06A, 06B, and 06C
- ▶ Blocks 08A, 08B, and 08C
- ▶ Blocks 17A, 17B, and 17C
- ▶ Blocks 18A, 18B, and 18C
- ▶ Blocks 19A, 19B, and 19C
- ▶ Blocks 20A, 20B, and 20C
- ▶ Blocks 22A, 22B, and 22C
- ▶ Blocks 27A, 27B, and 27C
- ▶ Blocks 29A, 29B, and 29C

Use matching pieces to make pairs of 2 quadrants from the following blocks:

- ▶ Blocks 05B and 05C
- ▶ Blocks 20B and 20C
- ▶ Blocks 21A and 21B

Use the single pieces for the remaining quarter-circles:

- ▶ Block 05A
- ▶ Block 20A
- ▶ Block 21C

5. Referring to the quilt assembly diagram, arrange the blocks in rows. Sew the blocks in each row together.

6. Sew the rows together to complete the quilt top.

Quilt assembly

Finishing the Quilt

Sew the backing sections together to make a 68″ × 68″ square for the backing. Layer, baste, quilt, and bind as desired. Quilter Angela Walters created a lot of contrast between quilt elements by stitching soft, curvy patterns in some arcs and sharp linear designs in other areas.

Crazy Tula
PILLOWS

COORDINATING PILLOWS: 19″ diameter × 4″

MATERIALS ▸▸▸

Fabric and filling

Red pillow

ASSORTED FOCUS PRINTS:
8 fat eighths, ranging from
red to orange

LINEN SOLID: ½ yard

YELLOW PRINT: ½ yard

BACKING: ⅝ yard

POLYESTER FIBERFILL: 1 pound

Green pillow

ASSORTED FOCUS PRINTS:
8 fat eighths, ranging from
yellow to blue

CREAM SOLID: ⅜ yard

LINEN SOLID: 1 fat eighth

BLUE PRINT: ⅜ yard

BACKING: ⅝ yard

POLYESTER FIBERFILL: 1 pound

Purple pillow

ASSORTED FOCUS PRINTS:
8 fat eighths, ranging from
blue to violet

GREEN PRINT 1: ⅓ yard

GREEN PRINT 2: 1 fat eighth

BLUE PRINT: ⅜ yard

LINEN SOLID: 1 fat eighth

BACKING: ⅝ yard

POLYESTER FIBERFILL: 1 pound

Foundations and patterns

*Refer to Foundation-Pieced Arc Patterns (page 84) and Circle,
Background, and Plain Arc Patterns (page 93). Photocopy the number
of paper-piecing foundations listed. From template plastic, make a
template for the circle pattern.*

Red pillow

ARC B: 4

ARC D: 4

ARC F: 4

CIRCLE PATTERN: J1

Green pillow

ARC D: 4

ARC F: 4

CIRCLE AND ARC
PATTERNS: J1 and M

Purple pillow

ARC C: 4

ARC E: 4

CIRCLE AND ARC
PATTERNS: J1 and L

CUTTING ▶▶▶

For detailed cutting instructions, refer to Cutting Pieces for the Blocks (page 11).

RED PILLOW

Assorted focus prints

From each fat eighth:

- Cut 2 B squares. Subcut each on the diagonal once.
- Cut 4 D rectangles.
- Cut 4 F rectangles.

Linen solid

- Cut 32 B squares. Subcut each on the diagonal once.

Yellow print

- Cut 2 rectangles 4½″ × 30⅜″.
- Cut 1 J1 circle.

Backing

- Cut 1 square 21″ × 21″.

GREEN PILLOW

Assorted focus prints

From each fat eighth:

- Cut 4 D rectangles.
- Cut 4 F rectangles.

Cream solid

- Cut 4 M arcs.

Linen solid

- Cut 1 J1 circle.

Blue print

- Cut 2 rectangles 4½″ × 30⅜″.

Backing

- Cut 1 square 21″ × 21″.

PURPLE PILLOW

Assorted focus prints

From each fat eighth:

- Cut 2 C squares. Subcut each on the diagonal once.
- Cut 4 E rectangles.

Green print 1

- Cut 4 L arcs.

Green print 2

- Cut 1 J1 circle.

Blue print

- Cut 2 rectangles 4½″ × 30⅜″.

Linen solid

- Cut 32 C squares. Subcut each on the diagonal once.

Backing

- Cut 1 square 21″ × 21″.

Pillow Construction

1. Using the techniques in Quilt Construction, Steps 1–3 (page 46), sew pieced and plain arcs together to complete 4 quarter-circles from Blocks 05, 18, or 21 for 1 pillow, or you can make 4 quarter-circles from each to make all 3 pillows. To make the round pillows, do not add the K background pieces. Sew the blocks together to complete the round pillow top.

2. Refer to Finishing the Pillows (page 18) to learn how to assemble the pillows.

Seeing Spots

FINISHED QUILT: 42½″ × 56½″
FINISHED BLOCK (QUARTER-CIRCLE): 10″ × 10″

Designed and made by Carl Hentsch, quilted by Mary Verstraete Honas, 2016
Fabrics: Spots and Kaffe Classics by Kaffe Fassett for Westminster Fibers

This was one of the last quilts for which we chose the fabrics. Tula and I were discussing what was missing from the color-story progression through the book. We were looking though fabric samples, and we both looked up and said, "Kaffe Spots."

Once we were able to choose the 32 fabrics for the blocks we knew that the background for the Flying Geese had to be "plain." But instead of choosing a solid, I found a tone-on-tone print with polka dots that matched the size of the other spots.

Trying to determine what was missing from the color story within this quilt, we decided on a base of yellow for the background. The fabrics are mainly yellow but also carry the color theme from the spots. We chose a coordinating stripe for the binding.

MATERIALS ▸▸▸

These materials are for the quilt. To make a pillow, see Seeing Spots Pillows (page 54). Yardages are based on 42˝ usable width.

ASSORTED POLKA-DOT BRIGHT PRINTS:
32 fat eighths for pieced arcs

NEUTRAL POLKA-DOT TONE-ON-TONE PRINT:
1 yard for Flying Geese backgrounds

SMALL-SCALE PRINT: ¾ yard for block backgrounds and quarter-circles

LARGE-SCALE FLORAL PRINT: 2⅛ yards for quilt setting blocks and center block circle

MULTICOLOR STRIPE: ⅜ yard for binding

BACKING: 2⅞ yards

BATTING: Twin-size

Foundations and patterns

Refer to Foundation-Pieced Arc Patterns (page 84) and Circle, Background, and Plain Arc Patterns (page 93). Photocopy the number of paper-piecing foundations listed. From template plastic, make templates for the circle and background patterns.

ARC A: 4   ARC H: 4

ARC C: 6   CIRCLE AND BACKGROUND

ARC G: 6   PATTERNS: J1, J3, and K

CUTTING ▸▸▸

For detailed cutting instructions, refer to Cutting Pieces for the Blocks (page 11).

ASSORTED POLKA-DOT BRIGHT PRINTS
Before you start cutting, divide the fat-eighth fabrics into general color groups. Arrange the fabrics in a circle, with each fabric color flowing into the next. Choose a fabric anywhere in the circle and label it Fabric 1. Working clockwise around the circle, label the rest of the fabrics 2–32.

Fabrics 1–8
From each fat eighth:

- Cut 1 A square and 1 C square.
  Subcut each on the diagonal once.

- Cut 1 G rectangle.

- Cut 1 H rectangle.

Fabrics 9–16
From each fat eighth:

- Cut 1 A square and 1 C square.
  Subcut each on the diagonal once.

- Cut 2 G rectangles.

- Cut 1 H rectangle.

Fabrics 17–24
From each fat eighth:

- Cut 1 A square and 1 C square.
  Subcut each on the diagonal once.

- Cut 1 G rectangle.

- Cut 1 H rectangle.

Fabrics 25–32
From each fat eighth:

- Cut 1 A square and 1 C square.
  Subcut each on the diagonal once.

- Cut 2 G rectangles.

- Cut 1 H rectangle.

NEUTRAL POLKA-DOT TONE-ON-TONE PRINT
- Cut 32 A squares and 48 C squares.
  Subcut each on the diagonal once.

Cutting list continues …

Cutting list continued ...

SMALL-SCALE PRINT

- Cut 10 K and 10 K-reverse backgrounds.

- Cut 6 J3 quarter-circles.

LARGE-SCALE FLORAL PRINT

- Cut 8 squares 10½″ × 10½″.

- Cut 3 squares 15½″ × 15½″. Subcut each on the diagonal twice to yield 12 setting triangles. You will need 10.

- Cut 2 squares 8″ × 8″. Subcut each on the diagonal once to yield 4 corner triangles.

- Fussy cut 1 J1 circle.

BINDING

- Cut enough 2¼″ bias strips to make 208″ of bias binding.

BACKING

- Cut 2 pieces 51″ × width of fabric.

Quilt Construction

To see how the blocks are assembled, refer to Block Index (page 76). For foundation- and curved-piecing techniques, refer to Making the Blocks (page 10).

1. Match the fabric pieces by letter with the printed foundations for the arcs. Foundation piece 4 each of Arcs A and H, which you should label quadrants A, B, C, and D. Use the colors in order so that when the blocks are sewn together to make a circle, the color flows around the circle from quadrant to quadrant. Use Fabrics 1–8 for quadrant A, Fabrics 9–16 for quadrant B, and so on.

2. In the same manner, foundation piece 6 each of Arcs C and G. You will not be able to use all 32 fabrics. Instead, piece the following for each arc pattern:

- ▶ Use Fabrics 1–8 to make 1 arc in Quadrant A fabrics.

- ▶ Use Fabrics 9–16 to make 2 arcs in Quadrant B fabrics.

- ▶ Use Fabrics 17–24 to make 1 arc in Quadrant C fabrics.

- ▶ Use Fabrics 25–32 to make 2 arcs in Quadrant D fabrics.

3. Combine Arcs A and H with the K and K-reverse backgrounds to make 4 of Block 07. Stitch the quadrants together. Appliqué the fussy-cut J1 full circle to the center to complete the full-circle block.

4. Combine Arcs C and G with the quarter-circle J3 and the K and K-reverse backgrounds to complete 6 of Block 06. Keep the quadrants labeled A, B, C, and D.

5. Referring to the quilt assembly diagram (next page), arrange the blocks in diagonal rows around the full-circle block. In each row, note the location of quadrants A–D. Sew small sections of triangles and squares together as shown in the assembly diagram.

6. Sew the pieced sections to the top right and bottom left side of the center full-circle block. Stitch the remaining sections together and add them to the top left and bottom right of the quilt center to complete the quilt top.

Quilt assembly

Finishing the Quilt

Sew the backing sections together and trim to 51″ × 65″. Layer, baste, quilt, and bind as desired. Mary Verstraete Honas let the sharp lines of the piecing do all the talking by simply quilting-in-the-ditch around the pieced arcs. She added a soft overall pattern to the background.

Seeing Spots
PILLOWS

COORDINATING PILLOWS: 19″ diameter × 4″

MATERIALS ▶▶▶

If you are making the quilt, you will have enough leftover fabric to make 1 pillow top. To make both pillows, you will need the following:

ASSORTED POLKA-DOT BRIGHT PRINTS:
32 fat eighths

NEUTRAL POLKA-DOT TONE-ON-TONE PRINT:
¾ yard

LARGE-SCALE FLORAL PRINT: ¾ yard for pillow sides and center circles

BACKING: ⅝ yard

POLYESTER FIBERFILL: 2 pounds

Foundations and patterns

Refer to Foundation-Pieced Arc Patterns (page 84) and Circle, Background, and Plain Arc Patterns (page 93). Photocopy the number of paper-piecing foundations listed. From template plastic, make a template for the circle pattern.

ARC A: 4	ARC H: 4
ARC C: 4	CIRCLE PATTERN: J1
ARC G: 4	

CUTTING ▸▸▸

For detailed cutting instructions, refer to Cutting Pieces for the Blocks (page 11).

ASSORTED POLKA-DOT BRIGHT PRINTS

Before you start cutting, divide the fat eighths into general color groups. Arrange the fabrics in a circle, with each fabric color flowing into the next. Choose a fabric anywhere in the circle and label it Fabric 1. Working clockwise around the circle, label the rest of the fabrics 2–32.

From each fat eighth:

• Cut 1 C square. Subcut on the diagonal once.

• Cut 1 G rectangle.

• Cut 1 H rectangle.

NEUTRAL POLKA-DOT TONE-ON-TONE PRINT

• Cut 32 A squares and 32 C squares. Subcut each on the diagonal once.

LARGE-SCALE FLORAL PRINT

• Cut 4 rectangles 4½″ × 30⅜″.

• Fussy cut 2 J1 circles.

BACKING

• Cut 2 squares 21″ × 21″.

Pillow Construction

1. Using the techniques in Quilt Construction, Steps 1–3 (page 52), sew pieced and plain arcs together to complete 4 of Block 06 and 4 of Block 07 for the 2 pillows. Use 1 set of the C square triangles for the Arc A Flying Geese. To make the round pillows, do not add the K background pieces.

2. Refer to Finishing the Pillows (page 18) to learn how to assemble the pillows.

Foxhole

FINISHED QUILT: 28⅓″ × 42½″
FINISHED BLOCK (QUARTER-CIRCLE): 10″ × 10″

This quilt started with the wonderful Chipper line by Tula Pink. We were able to select the coordinating solids ranging from gray to blue and ending in greens. The Flying Geese are high-lighted against the light gray, while the dark gray background allows the ring to almost pop off the quilt.

The large squares were a perfect place to use a large-scale print. Instead of using the same fabrics for the setting triangles, we chose a coordinating medium-scale print.

The quilt gets its name from the fox napping in the center that looks like it dug its burrow in the center of the quilt.

Designed and made by
Carl Hentsch, quilted by
Mary Verstraete Honas, 2016

Fabrics: Chipper by Tula Pink for
FreeSpirit Fabric and Designer
Basics by FreeSpirit Fabric

MATERIALS ▸▸▸

These materials are for the quilt. To make the pillow, see Foxhole Pillow (page 59). Yardages are based on 42″ usable width.

ASSORTED SOLIDS: 32 fat eighths for pieced arcs

LIGHT GRAY SMALL-SCALE PRINT: ½ yard for Flying Geese backgrounds

MEDIUM-SCALE FLORAL PRINT: ¾ yard for setting triangles and plain arcs

MEDIUM GRAY TONE-ON-TONE PRINT: ¼ yard for block backgrounds

LARGE-SCALE FLORAL PRINT: ⅝ yard for large squares

LARGE-SCALE PRINT: 1 fat quarter for block center circle

MULTICOLOR STRIPE: ⅜ yard for bias binding

BACKING: 2⅛ yards

BATTING: Crib-size

Foundations and patterns

Refer to Foundation-Pieced Arc Patterns (page 84) and Circle, Background, and Plain Arc Patterns (page 93). Photocopy the number of paper-piecing foundations listed. From template plastic, make templates for the circle, background, and arc patterns.

ARC B: 4	CIRCLE, BACKGROUND, AND ARC PATTERNS:
ARC F: 4	J1, K, and L

CUTTING ▸▸▸

For detailed cutting instructions, refer to Cutting Pieces for the Blocks (page 11).

ASSORTED SOLIDS

From each fat eighth:

- Cut 1 B square. Subcut on the diagonal once.
- Cut 1 F rectangle.

LIGHT GRAY SMALL-SCALE PRINT

- Cut 32 B squares. Subcut each on the diagonal once.

MEDIUM-SCALE FLORAL PRINT

- Cut 2 squares 15½″ × 15½″. Subcut each on the diagonal twice to yield 8 setting triangles. You will need 6.
- Cut 2 squares 8″ × 8″. Subcut each on the diagonal once to yield 4 corner triangles.
- Cut 4 L arcs.

MEDIUM GRAY TONE-ON-TONE PRINT

- Cut 4 K and 4 K-reverse backgrounds.

LARGE-SCALE FLORAL PRINT

- Cut 4 squares 10½″ × 10½″.

LARGE-SCALE PRINT

- Fussy cut 1 J1 circle.

BINDING

- Cut enough 2¼″ bias strips to make 152″ of bias binding.

BACKING

- Cut 2 pieces 37″ × width of fabric.

Quilt Construction

To see how the blocks are assembled, refer to Block Index (page 76). For foundation- and curved-piecing techniques, refer to Making the Blocks (page 10).

1. Keeping the assorted prints in their general color groups, arrange all the prints in a circle, with each fabric color flowing into the next. Choose a fabric anywhere in the circle and label it Fabric 1. Working clockwise around the circle, label the rest of the fabrics 2–32.

2. Match the fabric pieces by letter with the printed foundations for the arcs. Foundation piece 4 of Arc B and 4 of Arc F. In each arc, use Fabrics 1–8 for quadrant A, Fabrics 9–16 for quadrant B, and so on.

3. Arrange the pieced arcs with the L plain arcs and the K and K-reverse backgrounds to make 4 each of Block 17. Before you sew the arcs together, refer to the block layout diagram to rotate the B arcs a half-turn. For example, match the B arc from Fabrics 1–8 with the F arc from Fabrics 17–24, and the B arc from Fabrics 9–16 with the F arc from Fabrics 25–32.

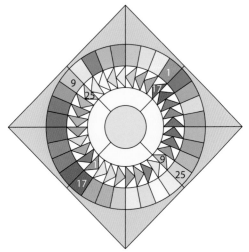

Block layout

4. Stitch the pieces in each quadrant together. Sew the quadrants together to make a full-circle block. To finish the circle, appliqué a J1 circle to the center of the block.

5. Referring to the quilt assembly diagram (at right), arrange the remaining squares and setting triangles in diagonal rows around the center block.

6. In the top right corner and the bottom left corner, sew the side setting triangle to the large square; then add the corner setting triangle. Stitch the units to the sides of the center block.

7. In the top left corner and lower right corner, sew a setting triangle to each side of the large square; then add the corner setting triangle. Stitch the units to the 2 remaining sides of the center block to complete the quilt top.

Quilt assembly

Finishing the Quilt

Sew the backing sections together and trim to make a 37″ × 51″ rectangle. Layer, baste, quilt, and bind as desired. Quilter Mary Verstraete Honas added another layer of interest by stitching Flying Geese in the inner and outer rings of the block. She highlighted the central block by quilting concentric rings throughout the remainder of the quilt.

Foxhole
PILLOW

COORDINATING PILLOW: 19″ diameter × 4″

MATERIALS ▸▸▸

If you are making the quilt, you will have enough leftover fabric to make the pillow top.

ASSORTED SOLIDS: 32 fat eighths

LIGHT GRAY SMALL-SCALE PRINT: ½ yard

MEDIUM-SCALE FLORAL PRINT: ¼ yard

LARGE-SCALE PRINT: 1 fat quarter for center circle

STRIPE: ⅜ yard for pillow sides

BACKING: ⅝ yard

POLYESTER FIBERFILL: 1 pound

Foundations and patterns

Refer to Foundation-Pieced Arc Patterns (page 84) and Circle, Background, and Plain Arc Patterns (page 93). Photocopy the number of paper-piecing foundations listed. From template plastic, make a template for the circle pattern.

ARC B: 4   ARC F: 4   CIRCLE PATTERN: J1

CUTTING ▸▸▸

For detailed cutting instructions, refer to Cutting Pieces for the Blocks (page 11).

ASSORTED SOLIDS

Before you start cutting, divide the fabrics into general color groups. Arrange the fabrics in a circle, with each fabric color flowing into the next. Choose a fabric anywhere in the circle and label it Fabric 1. Working clockwise around the circle, label the rest of the fabrics 2–32.

From each fat eighth:

- Cut 1 B square. Subcut on the diagonal once.
- Cut 1 F rectangle.

LIGHT GRAY SMALL-SCALE PRINT

- Cut 32 B squares. Subcut each on the diagonal once.

MEDIUM-SCALE FLORAL PRINT

- Cut 4 L arcs.

LARGE-SCALE PRINT

- Fussy cut 1 J1 circle.

STRIPE

- Cut 2 rectangles 4½″ × 30⅜″.

BACKING

- Cut 1 square 21″ × 21″.

Pillow Construction

1. Using the techniques in Quilt Construction, Steps 1–3 (page 57), sew together pieced and plain arcs to complete 4 quarter-circles from Block 17 for 1 pillow. To make the round pillow, do not add the K background pieces.

2. Refer to Finishing the Pillows (page 18) to learn how to assemble the pillow.

Sorbet
32 FLAVORS

FINISHED QUILT: 80˝ × 80˝

FINISHED BLOCK (QUARTER-CIRCLE): 10˝ × 10˝

On a stroll in Paris, I stumbled upon a small confection shop. The eatery had a variety of tasty desserts and, of course, sorbet. And what's better than a bowl of delicious sorbet?

I started this quilt with a great fat-quarter bundle. We chose a large print for the background fabric that contained many of the colors in the original fabric bundle.

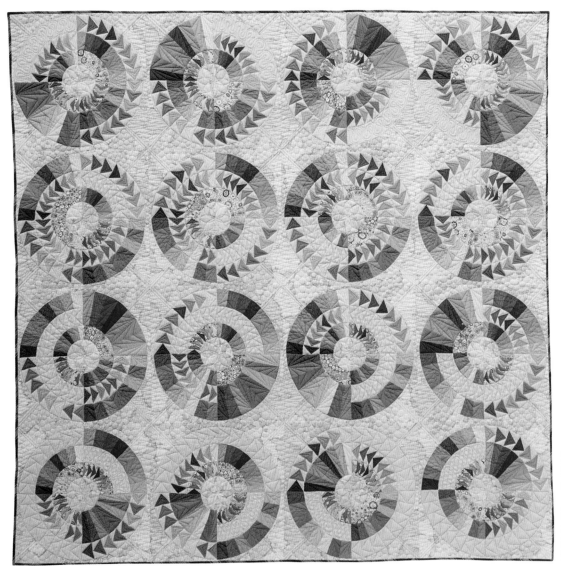

Designed and made by Carl Hentsch, quilted by Teresa Silva, 2016

Fabrics: Shot cottons and Kaffe Classics by Kaffe Fassett for Westminster Fibers

MATERIALS ▸▸▸

These materials are for the quilt. To make a pillow, see Sorbet Pillows (page 64). Yardages are based on 42˝ usable width.

ASSORTED SOLIDS: 32 fat quarters for pieced arcs

MEDIUM-SCALE PRINT: 1⅞ yards for inner plain arcs and Flying Geese backgrounds

POLKA-DOT PRINT: 2½ yards for center plain arcs and Flying Geese backgrounds

SMALL-SCALE PRINT: 3½ yards for outer plain arcs and Flying Geese backgrounds

LARGE-SCALE PRINT: 3¼ yards for block backgrounds and center circles

MULTICOLOR STRIPE: ⅝ yard for binding

BACKING: 7⅜ yards

BATTING: Queen-size

Foundations and patterns

Refer to Foundation-Pieced Arc Patterns (page 84) and Circle, Background, and Plain Arc Patterns (page 93). Photocopy the number of paper-piecing foundations listed. From template plastic, make templates for the circle, background, and arc patterns.

ARC A: 24	ARC F: 20
ARC B: 24	ARC G: 4
ARC C: 24	ARC H: 8
ARC D: 16	CIRCLE, BACKGROUND,
ARC E: 12	AND ARC PATTERNS: J3, K, L, M, and N

CUTTING ▸▸▸

For detailed cutting instructions, refer to Cutting Pieces for the Blocks (page 11).

ASSORTED SOLIDS
From each fat quarter:

- Cut 3 A squares, 3 B squares, and 3 C squares. Subcut each on the diagonal once.
- Cut 4 D rectangles.
- Cut 3 E rectangles.
- Cut 5 F rectangles.
- Cut 1 G rectangle.
- Cut 2 H rectangles.

MEDIUM-SCALE PRINT
- Cut 20 L arcs.
- Cut 192 A squares. Subcut each on the diagonal once.

POLKA-DOT PRINT
- Cut 16 M arcs.
- Cut 192 B squares. Subcut each on the diagonal once.

SMALL-SCALE PRINT
- Cut 12 N arcs.
- Cut 192 C squares. Subcut each on the diagonal once.

LARGE-SCALE PRINT
- Cut 64 K and 64 K-reverse backgrounds.
- Cut 64 J3 quarter-circles.

BINDING
- Cut enough 2¼˝ bias strips to make 330˝ of bias binding.

BACKING
- Cut 3 pieces 88˝ × width of fabric.

Quilt Construction

To see how the blocks are assembled, refer to Block Index (page 76). For foundation- and curved-piecing techniques, refer to Making the Blocks (page 10).

1. Divide the assorted solids into general color groups and then arrange the fabrics in a circle, with each fabric color flowing into the next. Choose a fabric anywhere in the circle and label it Fabric 1. Working clockwise around the circle, label the rest of the fabrics 2–32.

2. Match the fabric pieces by letter with the printed foundations for the arcs. Foundation piece the number of arcs listed in Foundations and Patterns (page 61) in sets of 4 arcs, which you should label quadrants A, B, C, and D. Start with Fabric 1; use Fabrics 1–8 for quadrant A, Fabrics 9–16 for quadrant B, and so on. Use the fabrics in exactly the same positions in all the sets of arcs.

3. Combine the pieced arcs with the J3 quarter-circle; L, M, and N plain arcs; and K and K-reverse backgrounds to complete 4 quadrants of the following blocks: 03, 04, 05, 06, 07, 09, 10, 11, 16, 17, 18, 20, 21, 22, 23, and 24. Keep the quadrant label with each completed quadrant.

> NOTE For this quilt, you will mix up the quadrants before arranging them into circles for the finished quilt. But for the purposes of color planning and sewing the quadrants, think of the 4 quadrants of each block pattern as a full circle.

4. Referring to the quilt assembly diagram (next page), arrange the block quadrants in rows. Sew the blocks in each row together.

5. Sew the rows together to complete the quilt top.

Quilt assembly

Finishing the Quilt

Sew the backing sections together and trim to make an 88″ × 88″ square.
Layer, baste, quilt, and bind as desired. Quilter Teresa Silver added even
more movement to the quilt by stitching Flying Geese in some plain arcs
and curvy lines in others. She disguised the true placement of the block
seamlines by quilting mock diagonal "seamlines" into the block backgrounds
and then alternating the fill pattern from block to block.

Sorbet
PILLOWS

COORDINATING PILLOWS: 19″ diameter × 4″

MATERIALS ▶▶▶

If you are making the quilt, you will have enough leftover fabric to make at least 1 pillow top. To make 4 pillows, you will need the following:

ASSORTED SOLIDS: 32 fat eighths

MEDIUM-SCALE PRINT: ½ yard

POLKA-DOT PRINT: ¾ yard

SMALL-SCALE PRINT: 1¼ yards

LARGE-SCALE PRINT: 1¼ yards for pillow sides and center circles

BACKING: 1¼ yards

POLYESTER FIBERFILL: 4 pounds

Foundations and patterns

Refer to Foundation-Pieced Arc Patterns (page 84) and Circle, Background, and Plain Arc Patterns (page 93). Photocopy the number of paper-piecing foundations listed. From template plastic, make templates for the circle and arc patterns.

ARC A: 8	ARC D: 4	CIRCLE AND ARC PATTERNS: J1 and N
ARC B: 8	ARC F: 4	
ARC C: 8	ARC G: 4	

CUTTING ▶▶▶

For detailed cutting instructions, refer to Cutting Pieces for the Blocks (page 11).

ASSORTED SOLIDS

From each fat eighth:

- Cut 1 A square, 1 B square, and 1 C square. Subcut each on the diagonal once.
- Cut 1 D rectangle.
- Cut 1 F rectangle.
- Cut 1 G rectangle.

MEDIUM-SCALE PRINT

- Cut 64 A squares. Subcut each on the diagonal once.

POLKA-DOT PRINT

- Cut 64 B squares. Subcut each on the diagonal once.

SMALL-SCALE PRINT

- Cut 4 N arcs.
- Cut 64 C squares. Subcut each on the diagonal once.

LARGE-SCALE PRINT

- Cut 8 rectangles 4½″ × 30⅜″.
- Fussy cut 4 J1 circles.

BACKING

- Cut 4 squares 21″ × 21″.

Pillow Construction

1. Using the techniques in Quilt Construction, Steps 1–3 (page 62), sew pieced and plain arcs together to complete 1 quadrant each of Blocks 03, 05, 06, or 11 for 1 pillow. Or you can make 4 quadrants of each to make all 4 pillows. To make the round pillows, do not add the K background pieces.

2. Refer to Finishing the Pillows (page 18) to learn how to assemble the pillows.

Papyrus

FINISHED QUILT: 60″ × 60″
FINISHED BLOCK (QUARTER-CIRCLE): 10″ × 10″

▶▶▶▶▶▶▶▶▶▶▶▶▶▶▶▶▶▶▶▶▶▶▶▶▶▶▶▶▶▶▶▶▶▶

Like a faded paper, the blocks in this quilt fade from dark gray to the lightest creams.

This quilt captures the entire story of this book in one quilt, but in neutrals. Starting with the darkest gray in the upper left, the blocks slowly transition to light grays, beiges, and creams, just as the quilts in the book transition from dark to full color to neutrals and finally white. I love how the center fabrics seem to disappear as they mix with the neutral background fabric. I didn't realize I had such an extensive collection of neutrals—the only fabrics I had to purchase for this quilt were the background fabrics for the Flying Geese units.

Designed and made by Carl Hentsch, quilted by Kelly Cline, 2015

Fabrics: Various neutrals from the quiltmaker's stash

MATERIALS ▶▶▶

These materials are for the quilt. To make a pillow, see Papyrus Pillows (page 70). Yardages are based on 42″ usable width.

This quilt is constructed from 9 groups of 8 fabrics each, ranging from dark gray to cream.

ASSORTED PRINTS: 8 fat eighths for each of the following 9 groups (72 total) for the pieced arcs

Group 1: Dark gray

Group 2: Medium gray

Group 3: Light gray

Group 4: Dark beige

Group 5: Medium beige

Group 6: Light beige

Group 7: Dark cream

Group 8: Medium cream

Group 9: Light cream

WHITE SOLID 1: 1 yard for Flying Geese backgrounds

WHITE SOLID 2: 1¼ yards for Flying Geese backgrounds

WHITE SOLID 3: 2 yards for Flying Geese backgrounds

LARGE-SCALE FLORAL PRINT: 2¼ yards for block backgrounds, quarter-circles, and binding

BACKING: 3⅞ yards

BATTING: Twin-size

Foundations and patterns

Refer to Foundation-Pieced Arc Patterns (page 84) and Circle, Background, and Plain Arc Patterns (page 93). Photocopy the number of paper-piecing foundations listed. From template plastic, make templates for the circle and background patterns.

ARC A: 16	ARC E: 4	ARC I: 4
ARC B: 16	ARC F: 8	CIRCLE AND BACK-GROUND PATTERNS: J3 and K
ARC C: 20	ARC G: 8	
ARC D: 8	ARC H: 4	

CUTTING ▶▶▶

For detailed cutting instructions, refer to Cutting Pieces for the Blocks (page 11).

ASSORTED PRINTS

Group 1
From each fat eighth:

- Cut 2 A squares and 2 C squares. Subcut each on the diagonal once.

- Cut 4 E rectangles.

Group 2
From each fat eighth:

- Cut 2 A squares, 2 B squares, and 2 C squares. Subcut each on the diagonal once.

Group 3
From each fat eighth:

- Cut 2 C squares. Subcut each on the diagonal once.

- Cut 4 G rectangles.

Group 4
From each fat eighth:

- Cut 2 B squares and 2 C squares. Subcut each on the diagonal once.

- Cut 4 D rectangles.

Group 5
From each fat eighth:

- Cut 2 A squares and 2 B squares. Subcut each on the diagonal once.

- Cut 4 F rectangles.

Group 6
From each fat eighth:

- Cut 2 B squares. Subcut each on the diagonal once.

- Cut 4 D rectangles and 4 F rectangles.

Cutting list continues …

Cutting list continued ...

ASSORTED PRINTS (cont.)

Group 7

From each fat eighth:

• Cut 2 C squares. Subcut each on the diagonal once.

• Cut 4 G rectangles.

Group 8

From each fat eighth:

• Cut 2 A squares. Subcut each on the diagonal once.

• Cut 4 H rectangles.

Group 9

From each fat eighth:

• Cut 4 I rectangles.

WHITE SOLID 1

• Cut 128 A squares. Subcut each on the diagonal once.

WHITE SOLID 2

• Cut 128 B squares. Subcut each on the diagonal once.

WHITE SOLID 3

• Cut 160 C squares. Subcut each on the diagonal once.

LARGE-SCALE FLORAL PRINT

• Cut 36 K and 36 K-reverse backgrounds.

• Cut 36 J3 quarter-circles.

• Cut 7 strips 2¼″ × width of fabric to make 250″ of binding.

BACKING

• Cut 2 pieces 68″ × width of fabric.

Quilt Construction

To see how the blocks are assembled, refer to Block Index (page 76). For foundation- and curved-piecing techniques, refer to Making the Blocks (page 10).

1. Keeping the assorted prints in their general color groups, arrange the fabrics for each group in a row, with each fabric color flowing into the next. Choose the first fabric and label it Fabric 1. Working from left to right, label the rest of the fabrics 2–8.

2. Match the fabric pieces by letter with the printed foundations for the arcs. Foundation piece the number of arcs listed in Foundations and Patterns (page 67) in sets of 4 identical arcs each. Use the colors in exactly the same positions in all the arcs.

3. Combine the pieced arcs with the J3 quarter-circles and K and K-reverse backgrounds to complete 4 identical quadrants of Blocks 01, 02, 03, 04, 05, 07, and 08, and 2 sets of 4 identical quadrants of Block 06.

Use the following fabric groups to make the blocks:

▶ **Group 1:** Block 03

▶ **Group 2:** Block 01

▶ **Group 3:** Block 06

▶ **Group 4:** Block 02

▶ **Group 5:** Block 04

▶ **Group 6:** Block 05

▶ **Group 7:** Block 06

▶ **Group 8:** Block 07

▶ **Group 9:** Block 08

4. Referring to the quilt assembly diagram (next page), arrange the block quadrants in rows. Sew the blocks in each row together.

5. Sew the rows together to complete the quilt top.

Quilt assembly

Finishing the Quilt

Sew the backing sections together to make a 68″ × 68″ square for the backing.
Layer, baste, quilt, and bind as desired. Quilter Kelly Cline stitched a tight spiral
in the center of each full circle, added a variety of straight and curved designs
that followed the lines of the pieced arcs, and then finished the outside of each
circle with a row of gradated dots and a striking corner design.

Papyrus
PILLOWS

COORDINATING PILLOWS: 19″ diameter × 4″

MATERIALS ▶▶▶

To make all 3 pillows, each from a separate fabric group, you will need the following:

ASSORTED PRINTS:
8 fat eighths for each of
3 groups (24 total) for arcs

Group 1: Dark gray

Group 2: Medium beige

Group 3: Light cream

White solid 1: ½ yard

White solid 2: ½ yard

White solid 3: ⅝ yard

LARGE-SCALE FLORAL PRINT: ⅞ yard for sides and circle centers

BACKING: 1¼ yards

POLYESTER FIBERFILL:
3 pounds

Foundations and patterns

Refer to Foundation-Pieced Arc Patterns (page 84) and Circle, Background, and Plain Arc Patterns (page 93). Photocopy the number of paper-piecing foundations listed. From template plastic, make a template for the circle pattern.

ARC A: 8

ARC B: 4

ARC C: 4

ARC E: 4

ARC F: 4

ARC I: 4

CIRCLE PATTERN: J1

CUTTING ▶▶▶

For detailed cutting instructions, refer to Cutting Pieces for the Blocks (page 11).

ASSORTED PRINTS

Group 1

From each fat eighth:

- Cut 2 A squares and 2 C squares. Subcut each on the diagonal once.
- Cut 4 E rectangles.

Group 2

From each fat eighth:

- Cut 2 A squares and 2 B squares. Subcut each on the diagonal once.
- Cut 4 F rectangles.

Group 3

From each fat eighth:

- Cut 4 I rectangles.

WHITE SOLID 1

- Cut 64 A squares. Subcut each on the diagonal once.

WHITE SOLID 2

- Cut 32 B squares. Subcut each on the diagonal once.

WHITE SOLID 3

- Cut 32 C squares. Subcut each on the diagonal once.

LARGE-SCALE FLORAL PRINT

- Cut 6 rectangles 4½″ × 30⅜″ for the pillow sides.
- Cut 3 J1 circles.

BACKING

- Cut 3 squares 21″ × 21″.

Pillow Construction

1. Using the techniques in Quilt Construction, Steps 1–3 (page 68), sew pieced arcs together to complete 4 quarter-circles from Block 03, 04, or 08 for 1 pillow, or you can make 4 quarter-circles from each to make all 3 pillows.

Make the blocks in the following fabrics:

▶ **Group 1:** Block 03

▶ **Group 2:** Block 04

▶ **Group 3:** Block 08

To make the round pillows, do not add the K background pieces.

2. Refer to Finishing the Pillows (page 18) to learn how to assemble the pillows.

Wedding Cake

FINISHED QUILT: approx. 56½˝ × 56½˝
FINISHED BLOCK (QUARTER-CIRCLE): 10˝ × 10˝

A perfect wedding or anniversary gift in whites and off-whites, reminiscent of a tiered wedding cake. You won't have to worry about leaving this out in the rain. I have always wanted to make a quilt of neutral fabrics, but I never imagined that I would be making one of all white. It's a quilter's delight to add detailed quilting designs that enhance the piecing and really make it special.

Designed and made by Carl Hentsch, quilted by Karen McTavish, 2016

Fabrics: Miscellaneous fabrics from the quiltmaker's stash

MATERIALS ▸▸▸

These materials are for the quilt. To make a pillow, see Wedding Cake Pillow (page 75). Yardages are based on 42″ usable width.

ASSORTED WHITE PRINTS: ½ yard each of 8 different prints for pieced arcs (Choose tone-on-tone small-scale prints.)

SOLID WHITE 1: 1¼ yards for Arc A Flying Geese backgrounds

SOLID WHITE 2: 1¾ yards for Arc B Flying Geese backgrounds

SOLID WHITE 3: 2⅜ yards for Arc C Flying Geese backgrounds

LARGE-SCALE WHITE TONE-ON-TONE PRINT: 2⅛ yards for block backgrounds, setting triangles, and quarter-circles

WHITE STRIPE: ½ yard for bias binding

BACKING: 3⅝ yards

BATTING: Twin-size

Foundations and patterns

Refer to Foundation-Pieced Arc Patterns (page 84) and Circle, Background, and Plain Arc Patterns (page 93). Photocopy the number of paper-piecing foundations listed. From template plastic, make templates for the circle and background patterns.

ARC A: 24

ARC B: 24

ARC C: 24

CIRCLE AND BACK-GROUND PATTERNS:
J3 and K

CUTTING ▸▸▸

For detailed cutting instructions, refer to Cutting Pieces for the Blocks (page 11).

ASSORTED WHITE PRINTS
From each ½ yard:

- Cut 12 A squares, 12 B squares, and 12 C squares. Subcut each on the diagonal once.

WHITE SOLID 1

- Cut 192 A squares. Subcut each on the diagonal once.

WHITE SOLID 2

- Cut 192 B squares. Subcut each on the diagonal once.

WHITE SOLID 3

- Cut 192 C squares. Subcut each on the diagonal once.

LARGE-SCALE WHITE TONE-ON-TONE PRINT

- Cut 4 squares 15½″ × 15½″. Subcut each on the diagonal twice to yield 16 setting triangles.

- Cut 24 K and 24 K-reverse backgrounds.

- Cut 24 J3 quarter-circles.

BINDING

- Cut enough 2¼″ bias strips to make 236″ of bias binding.

BACKING

- Cut 2 pieces 65″ × width of fabric.

Quilt Construction

To see how the blocks are assembled, refer to Block Index (page 76). For foundation- and curved-piecing techniques, refer to Making the Blocks (page 10).

1. Arrange the assorted white prints in a row, starting with the lightest fabric and gradating to the darkest. Label the fabrics 1–8.

Match the fabric pieces by letter with the printed foundations for the arcs. Foundation piece 24 of each arc. Use the fabrics in exactly the same order in each arc.

2. Combine the pieced arcs with the J3 quarter-circle and K and K-reverse backgrounds to complete 24 of Block 01.

3. Referring to the quilt assembly diagram (page 74), arrange the blocks and setting triangles in diagonal rows. Sew the blocks and setting triangles in each diagonal row together.

4. Sew the rows together to complete the quilt top.

Quilt assembly

Finishing the Quilt

Sew the backing sections together and trim to make a 65″ × 65″
square for the quilt back. Layer, baste, quilt, and bind as desired.
Karen McTavish kept the quilting simple in the pieced arcs by
following the piecing lines, but she added an intricate feather
design in the block centers and drew a spectacular scrollwork
design in the quilt background that really makes the quilt sing.

Wedding Cake
PILLOW

COORDINATING PILLOW: 19˝ diameter × 4˝

MATERIALS ▸▸▸

If you are making the quilt, you will have enough leftover fabric to make at least 1 pillow top.

ASSORTED WHITE PRINTS: 1 fat eighth each of 8 different prints (Choose tone-on-tone small-scale prints.)

SOLID WHITE 1: ⅜ yard

SOLID WHITE 2: ⅜ yard

SOLID WHITE 3: ⅝ yard

WHITE TONE-ON-TONE LARGE-SCALE PRINT: ⅓ yard

BACKING: ⅝ yard

POLYESTER FIBERFILL: 1 pound

Foundations and patterns

Refer to Foundation-Pieced Arc Patterns (page 84) and Circle, Background, and Plain Arc Patterns (page 93). Photocopy the number of paper-piecing foundations listed. From template plastic, make a template for the circle pattern.

ARC A: 4   ARC C: 4

ARC B: 4   CIRCLE PATTERN: J1

CUTTING ▸▸▸

For detailed cutting instructions, refer to Cutting Pieces for the Blocks (page 11).

ASSORTED WHITE PRINTS
From each fat eighth:

- Cut 2 A squares, 2 B squares, and 2 C squares. Subcut each on the diagonal once.

WHITE SOLID 1

- Cut 32 A squares. Subcut each on the diagonal once.

WHITE SOLID 2

- Cut 32 B squares. Subcut each on the diagonal once.

WHITE SOLID 3

- Cut 32 C squares. Subcut each on the diagonal once.

WHITE TONE-ON-TONE LARGE-SCALE PRINT

- Cut 2 rectangles 4½˝ × 30⅜˝.

- Cut 1 J1 circle.

BACKING

- Cut 1 square 21˝ × 21˝.

Pillow Construction

1. Using the techniques in Quilt Construction, Steps 1–3 (page 73), sew pieced arcs together to complete 4 quarter-circles from Block 01. To make the round pillow, do not add the K background pieces.

2. Refer to Finishing the Pillows (page 18) to learn how to assemble the pillows.

Block Index

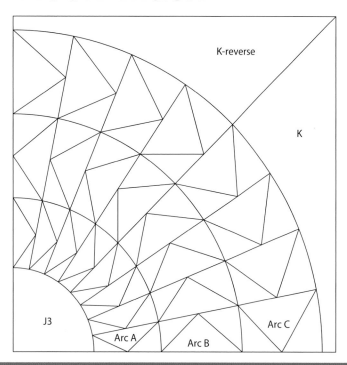

Block 01

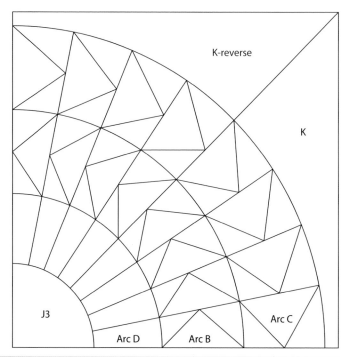

Block 02

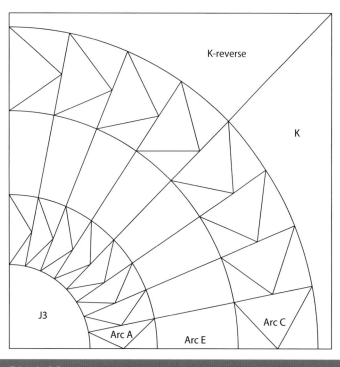

Block 03

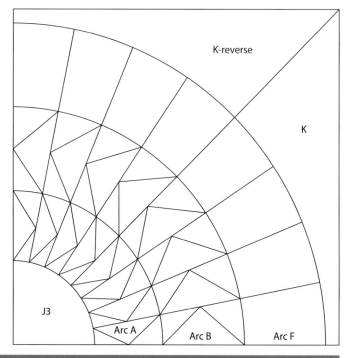

Block 04

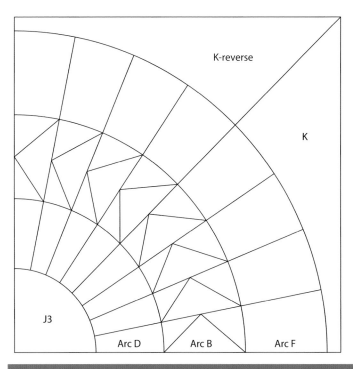

Block 05

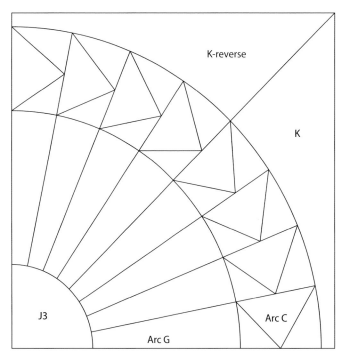

Block 06

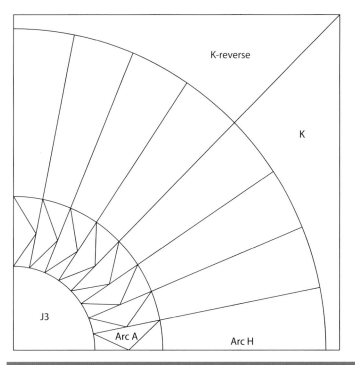

Block 07

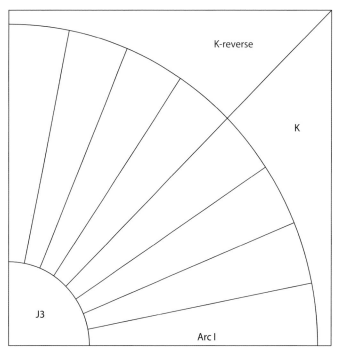

Block 08

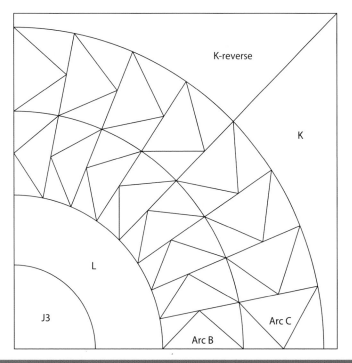

Block 09

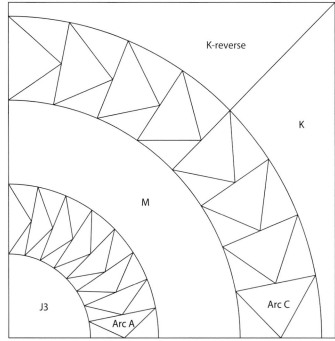

Block 10

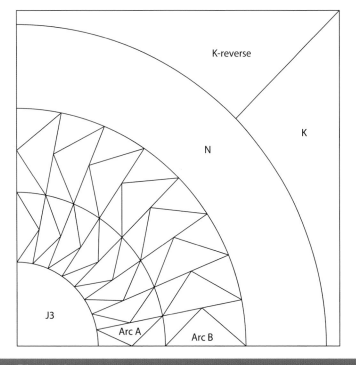

Block 11

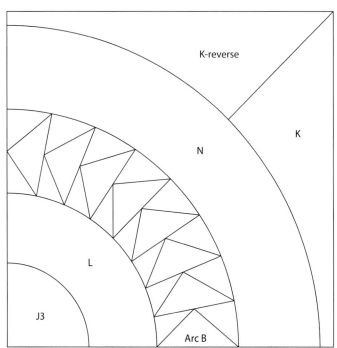

Block 12

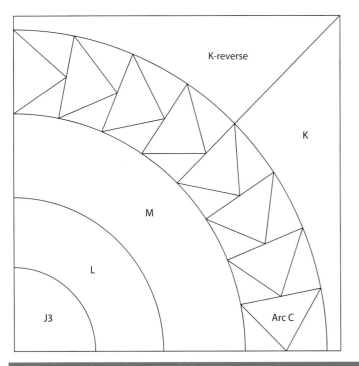

Block 13

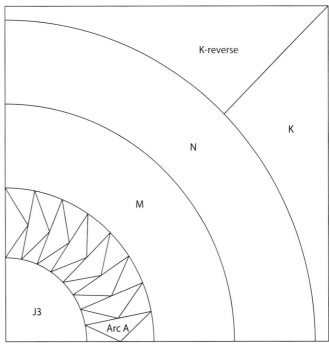

Block 14

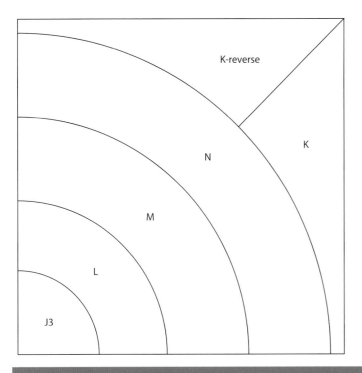

Block 15

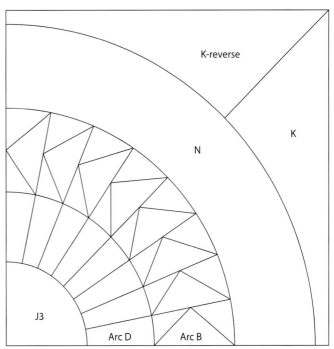

Block 16

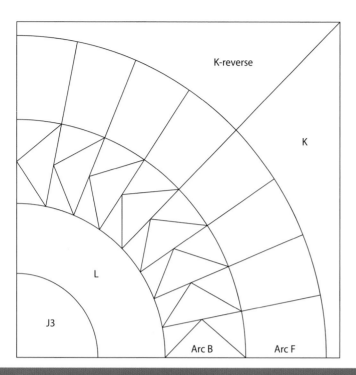

Block 17

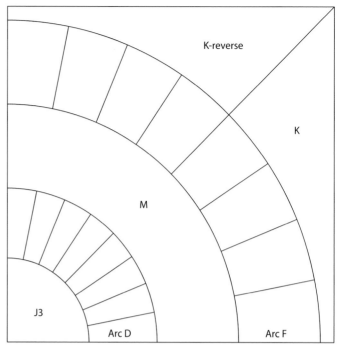

Block 18

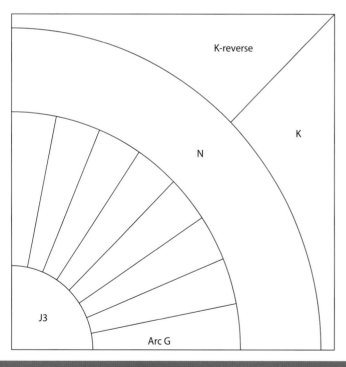

Block 19

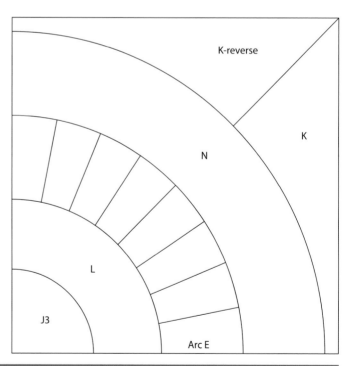

Block 20

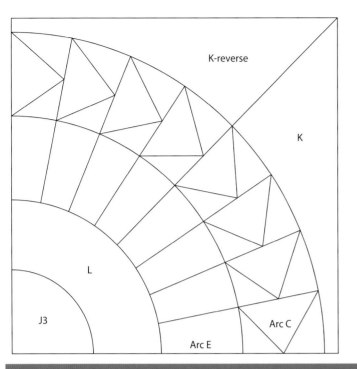

Block 21

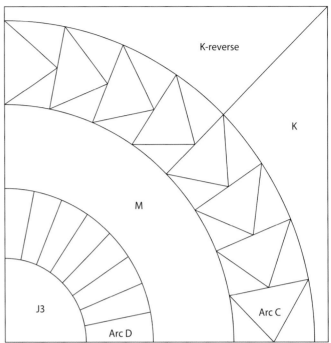

Block 22

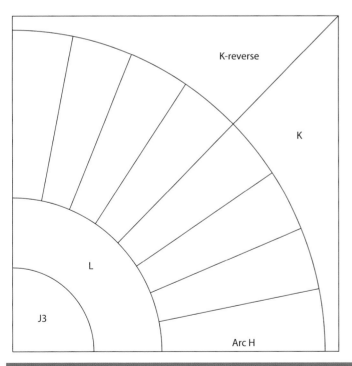

Block 23

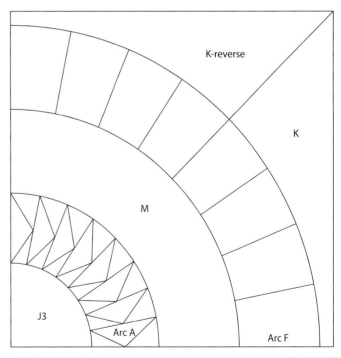

Block 24

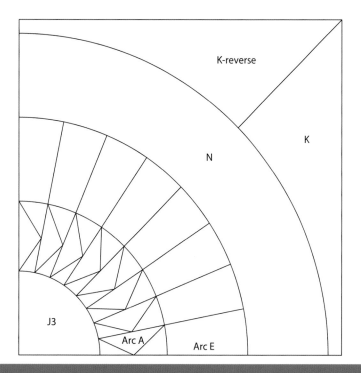

K-reverse

K

N

J3

Arc A

Arc E

Block 25

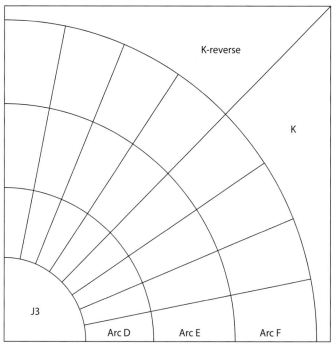

K-reverse

K

J3

Arc D

Arc E

Arc F

Block 26

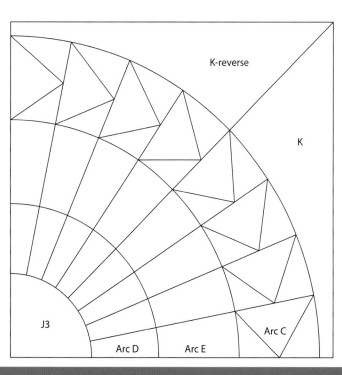

K-reverse

K

J3

Arc D

Arc E

Arc C

Block 27

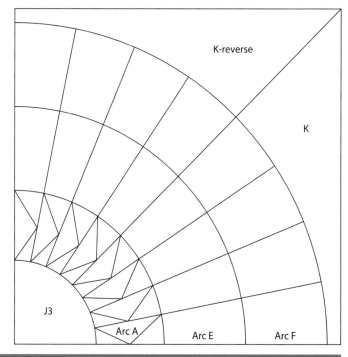

K-reverse

K

J3

Arc A

Arc E

Arc F

Block 28

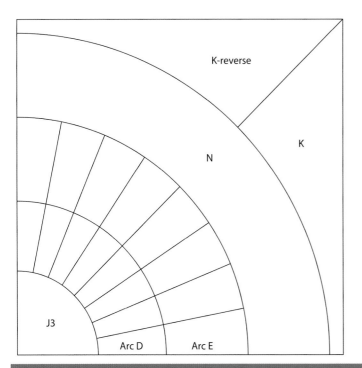

Block 29

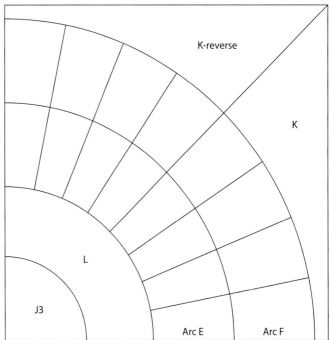

Block 30

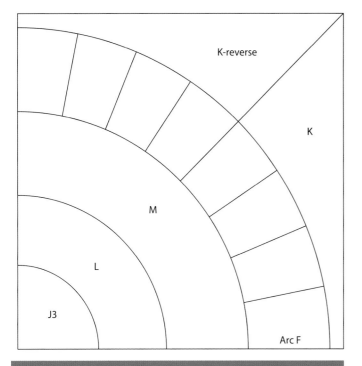

Block 31

Foundation-Pieced Arc Patterns

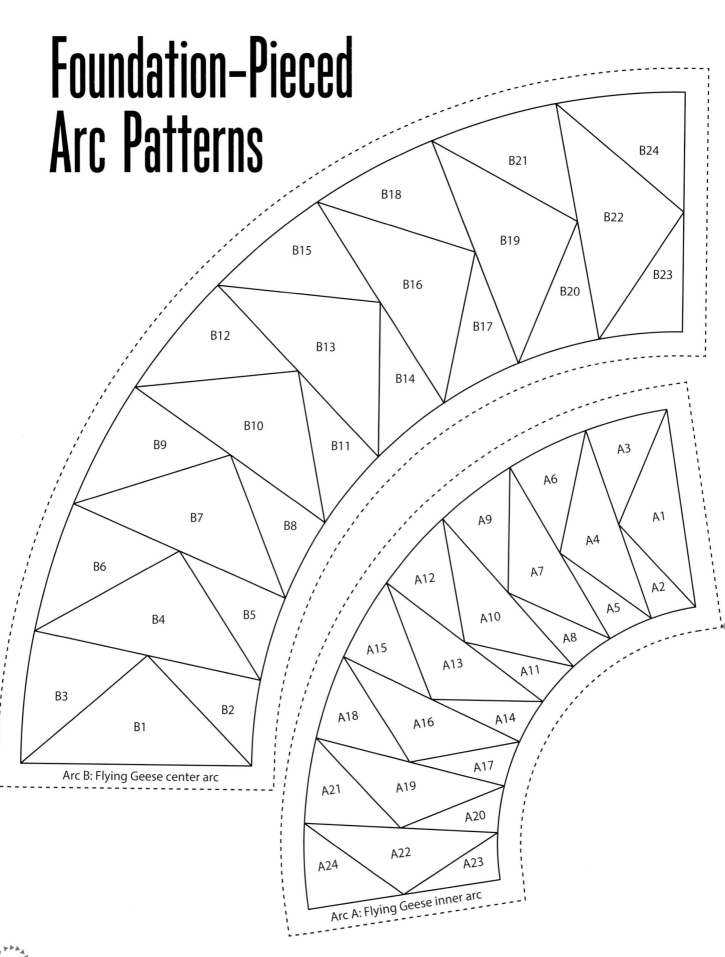

Arc B: Flying Geese center arc

Arc A: Flying Geese inner arc

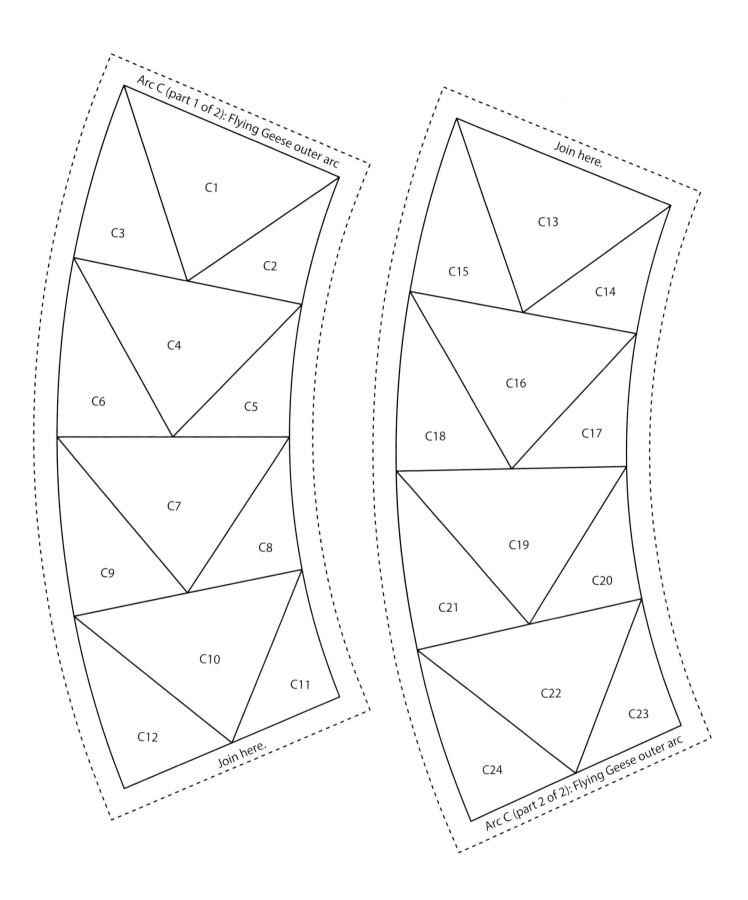

Arc C (part 1 of 2): Flying Geese outer arc

C1
C3
C2
C4
C6
C5
C7
C9
C8
C10
C11
C12

Join here.

Join here.

C13
C15
C14
C16
C18
C17
C19
C21
C20
C22
C23
C24

Arc C (part 2 of 2): Flying Geese outer arc

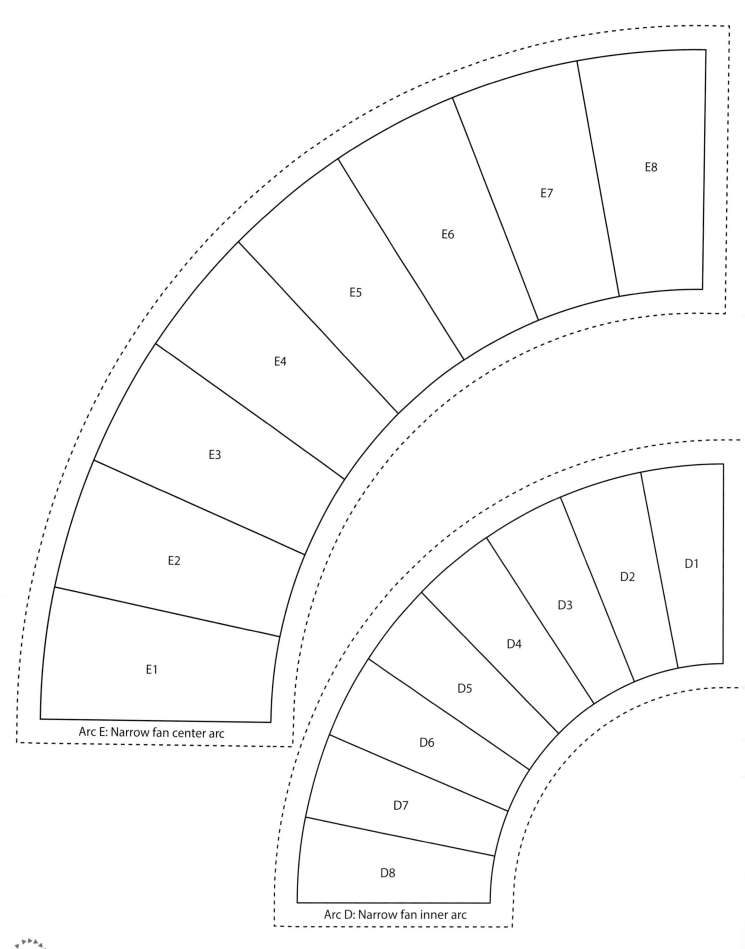

Arc E: Narrow fan center arc

Arc D: Narrow fan inner arc

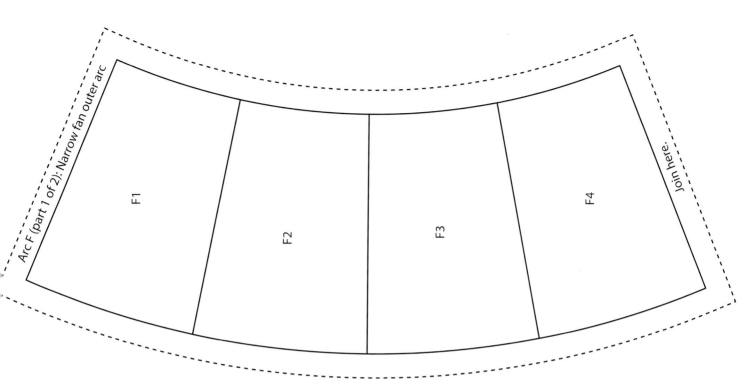

Arc F (part 1 of 2): Narrow fan outer arc

Join here.

F1

F2

F3

F4

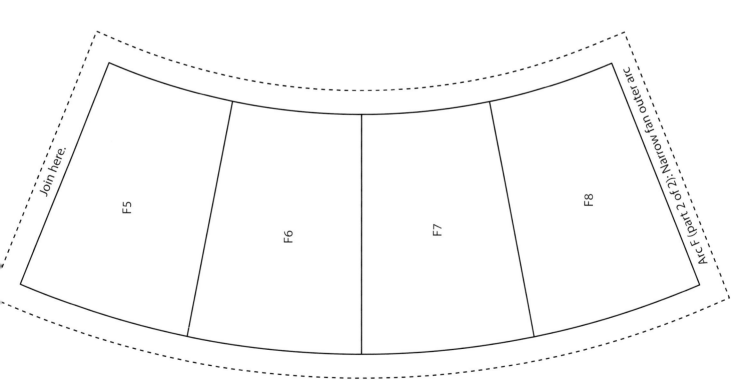

Join here.

Arc F (part 2 of 2): Narrow fan outer arc

F5

F6

F7

F8

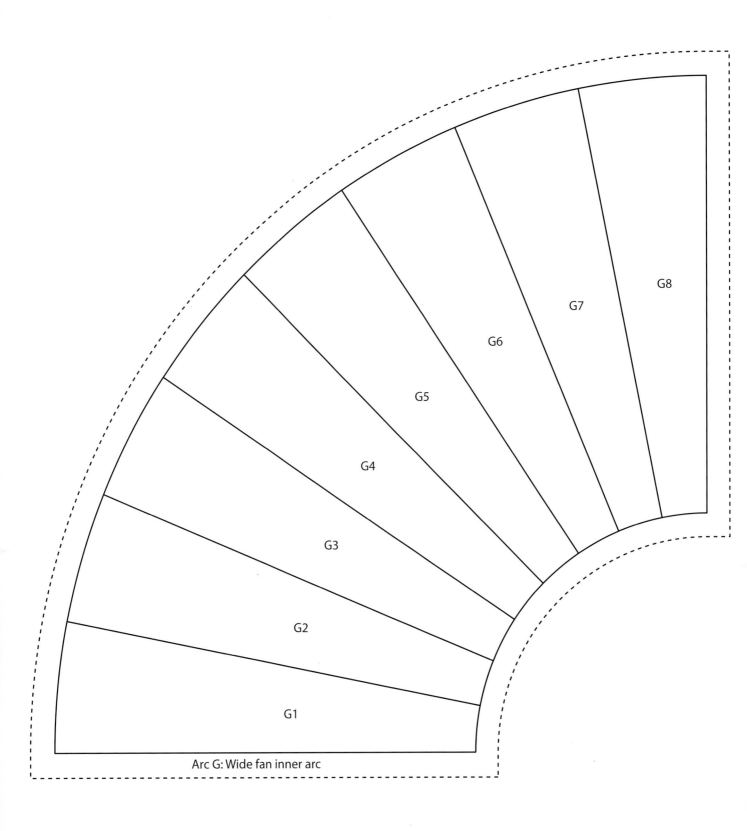

G8

G7

G6

G5

G4

G3

G2

G1

Arc G: Wide fan inner arc

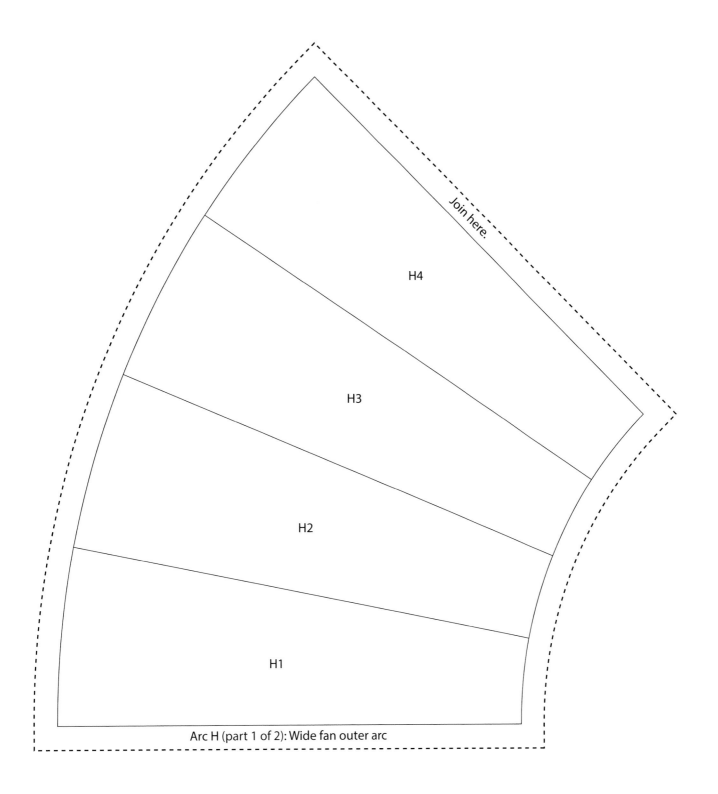

Join here.

H4

H3

H2

H1

Arc H (part 1 of 2): Wide fan outer arc

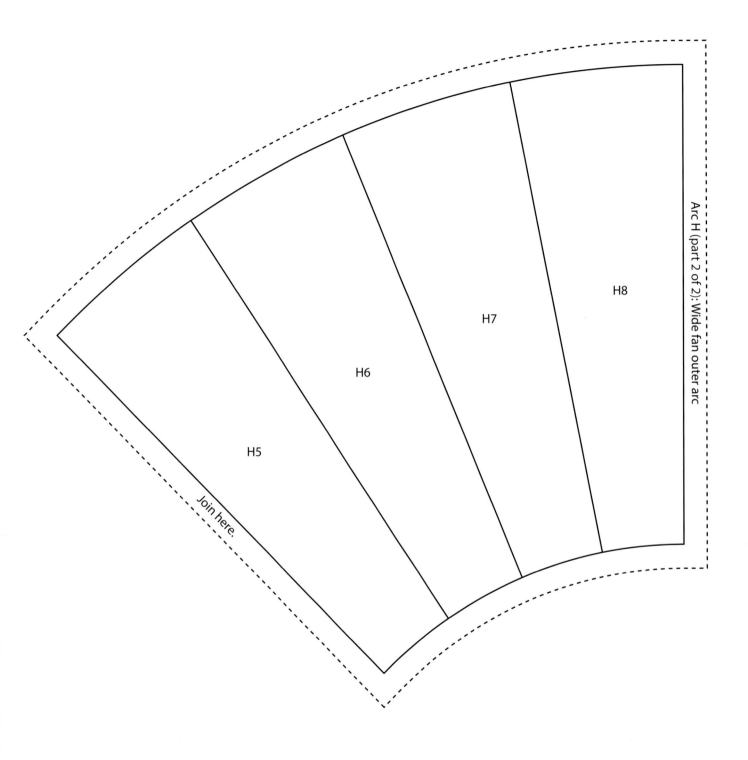

Arc H (part 2 of 2): Wide fan outer arc

H8

H7

H6

H5

Join here.

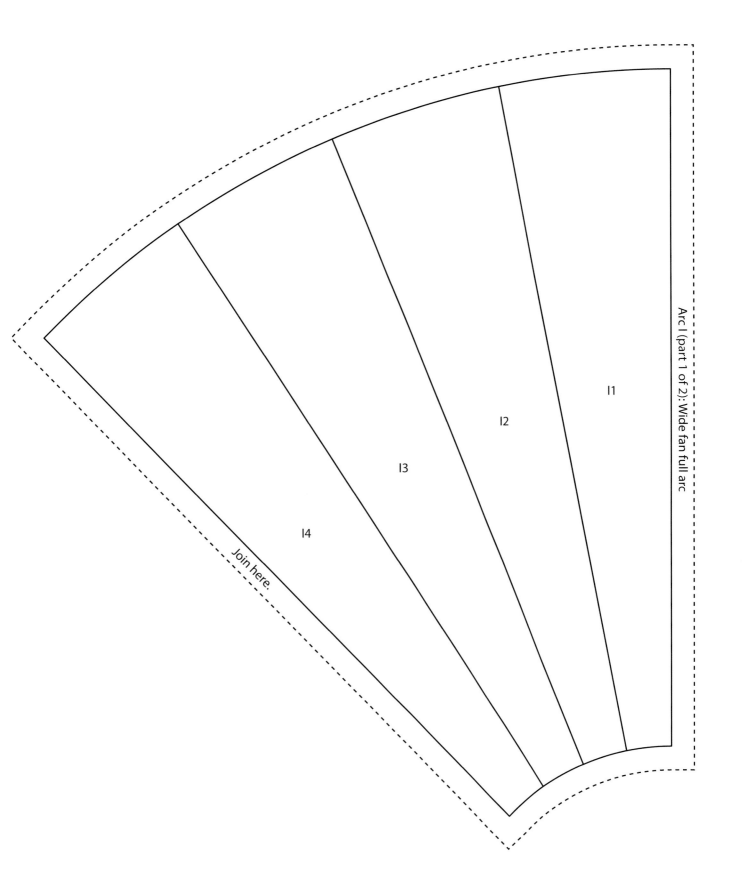

Arc I (part 1 of 2): Wide fan full arc

I1

I2

I3

I4

Join here.

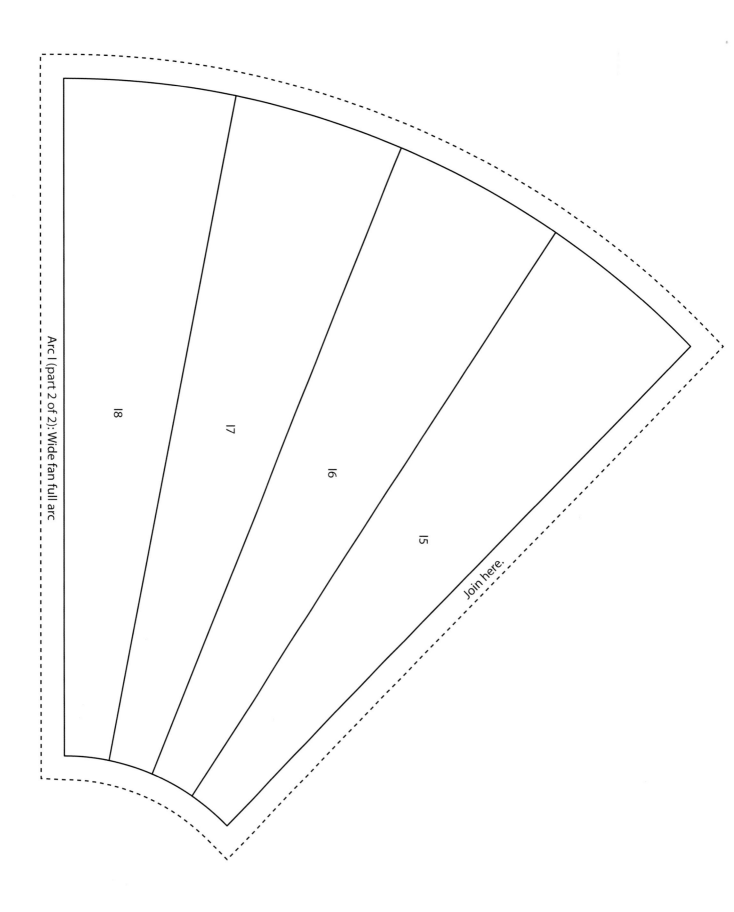

Arc I (part 2 of 2): Wide fan full arc

I8

I7

I6

I5

Join here.

Circle, Background, and Plain Arc Patterns

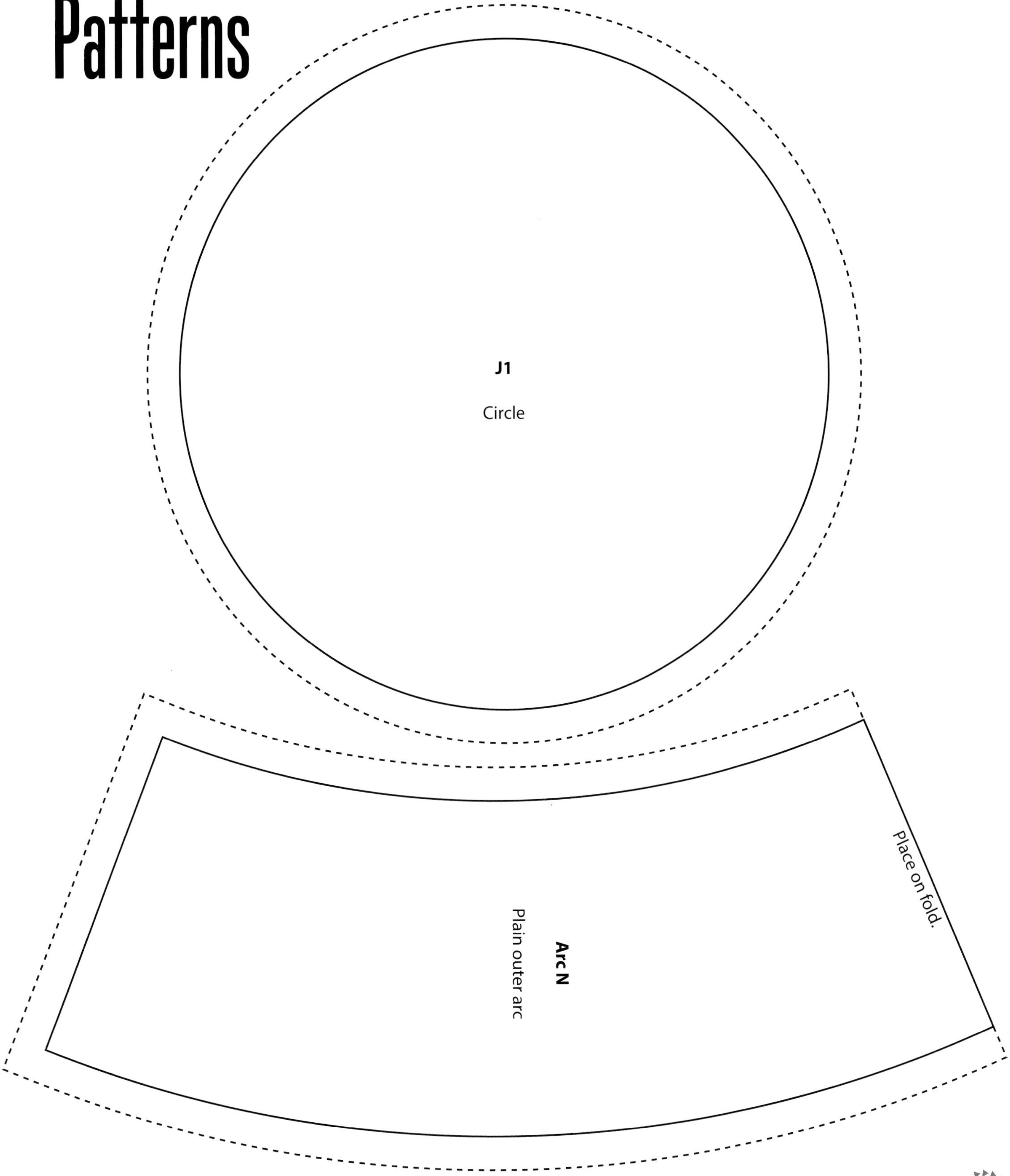

J1

Circle

Arc N

Plain outer arc

Place on fold.

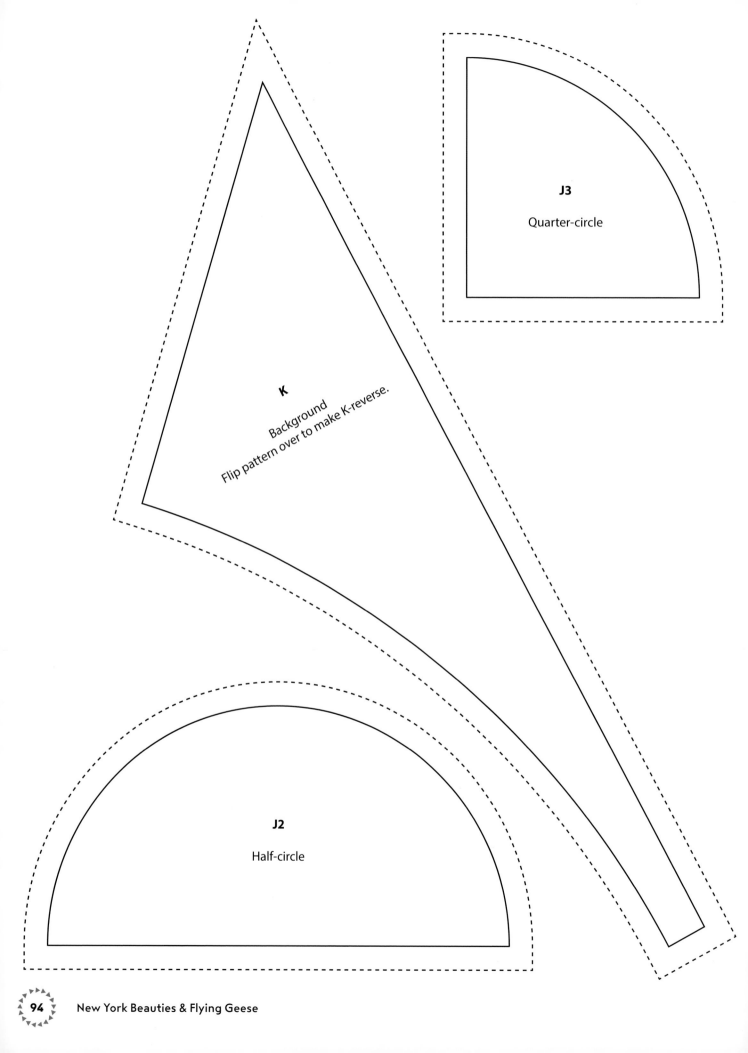

J3

Quarter-circle

K

Background

Flip pattern over to make K-reverse.

J2

Half-circle

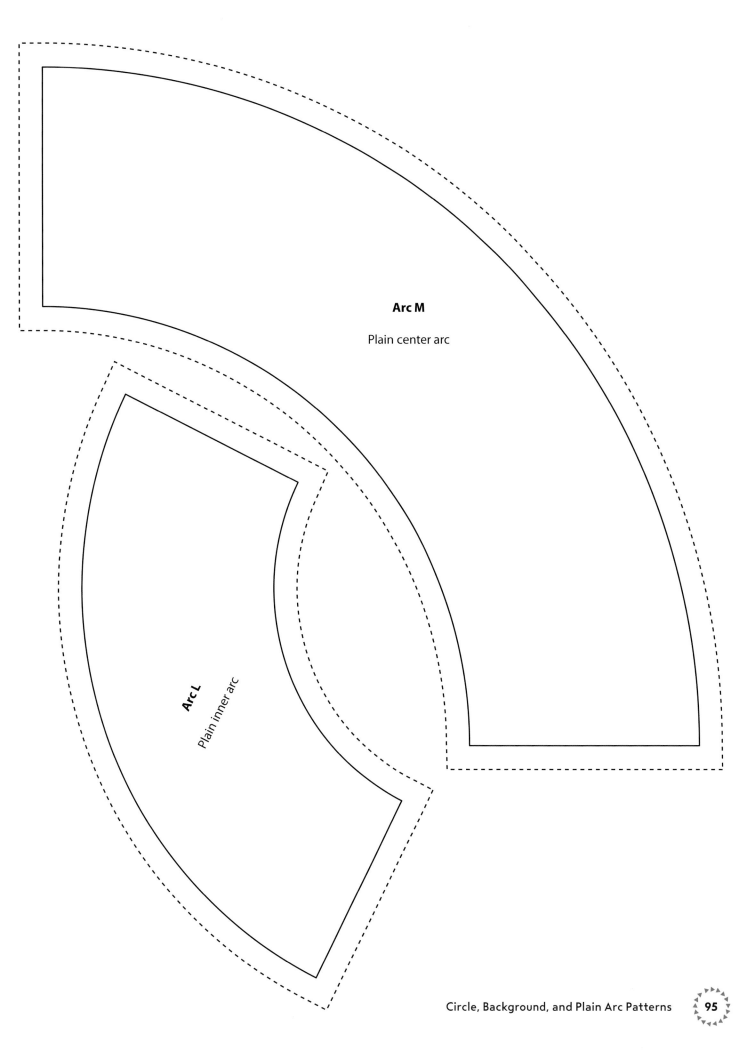

Arc M

Plain center arc

Arc L

Plain inner arc

About the Author

Photo by Mia Adams

Visit Carl's website at
3dogdesignco.com

Carl Hentsch taught himself quilting in 1997 after watching television shows such as *Simply Quilts*, *Quilt in a Day*, and *Love of Quilting*. He started to design his own quilts in 2006 and launched his design business in 2007. Carl's strong design sense is influenced by architecture and his two years spent living in Asia. In addition to designing quilts and writing books, Carl travels the country speaking and teaching at quilt guilds and quilt shops.

Born and raised on the beaches of Florida, Carl now lives in Missouri with his family of three dogs and a cat—Betty, Russel, Vivian, and Saffron. Carl has degrees in chemistry and biology from the University of Miami, a degree in linguistics from the Community College of the Air Force, and a degree in accounting and business management from the University of Central Florida.

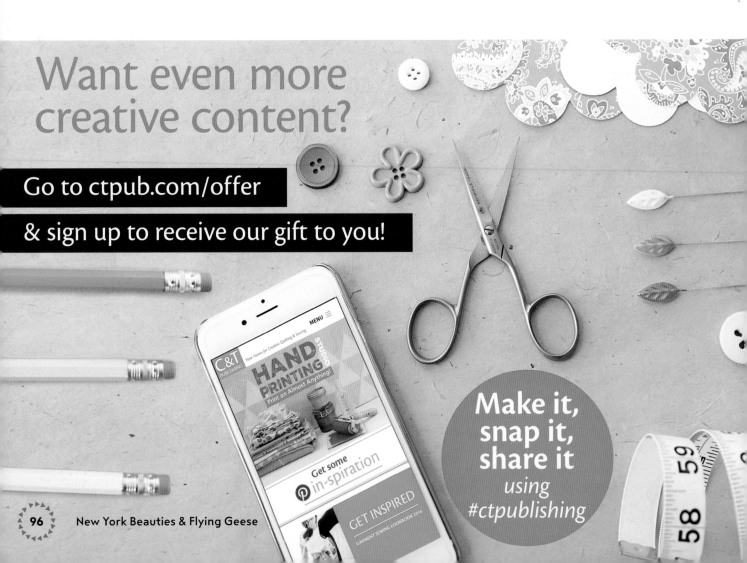

Want even more creative content?

Go to ctpub.com/offer

& sign up to receive our gift to you!

Make it, snap it, share it *using* #ctpublishing